M000097323

April 16, 1989

To Nancy,
    With best wishes and lots
of love in your future!

Jane

Finding Love

Creative strategies
for finding
your ideal mate

Finding
Love

Dr. Margaret O'Connor
and
Dr. Jane Silverman

Crown Publishers, Inc., New York

The quotes and excerpts from personal correspondence used in chapter 3 are from *Hands and Hearts—A History of Courtship in America* by Ellen Rothman, Basic Books, Inc., New York, 1984.

Copyright © 1989 by Margaret O'Connor and Jane Silverman

All rights reserved. No part of this book may be reproduced or transmitted in any form or by any means, electronic or mechanical, including photocopying, recording, or by any information storage and retrieval system, without permission in writing from the publisher.

Published by Crown Publishers, Inc., 225 Park Avenue South, New York, New York 10003

CROWN is a trademark of Crown Publishers, Inc.

Manufactured in the United States of America

Library of Congress Cataloging-in-Publication Data

O'Connor, Margaret (Margaret Rose)
   Finding love : creative strategies for finding your ideal mate
   Margaret O'Connor & Jane Silverman.
      p.   cm.
   1. Dating (Social customs)   2. Mate selection—United States.
   3. Single people—United States.   I. Silverman, Jane.   II. Title.
HQ801.O26 1989
646.7'7—dc19   88-18991

ISBN 0-517-57116-1

Design by Jake Victor Thomas

10   9   8   7   6   5   4   3   2   1

First Edition

Contents

Acknowledgments   *ix*

Introduction   *xi*

1. When Institutions Fail   3

Single and Looking   4

The Second Time Around   8

Finding Someone—The Demographic Dilemma   11

The Numbers Game—New Light on an Old
Problem   15

2. We Touched a Nerve   18

From the Sound of Many Voices   19

The Rise of the "Me" Generation   19

The Price of Cupid's Arrow—Cost vs. Reward   21

Great Expectations   23

Women with a Future   25

Jobless in Utopia   27

On Your Best Behavior—Changing Norms   28

Once a Jerk...   29

The Midas Syndrome   31

The Pay Date   32

The Prenuptial Agreement—Yours, Mine, and
Ours   34

3. Changing Expectations   36

Turning Back the Hands of Time   36

The Male–Female Split—There's No Place Like
Home?   38

Making Progress   41

Love on Wheels   43

Love in War and Peace   45

Revolution   46
Women's Lib—Look at Me Now   48
Tall, Dark, and Handsome   50

4. The New Intimacy   54
Then Came the Revolution   55
Pink Lady in a Red Dress   60
The Pill—Liberation in a Packet   61
Strangers in the Bedroom   63
Delilah with Muscles   68
Armageddon—The Reality of AIDS   70
Putting It Back Together   72
Rules for Intimacy   74

5. Methods and Madness   77
Making Up Your Own Rules   77
In the Good Old Days   80
Shame on You—The Girl Who Sent Herself a
    Valentine   81
The Fixer-Uppers—Informal Matchmakers   83
If You Can't Find It in the Yellow Pages—
    Advertise   85
Successful Advertising—Rules for the Personals   91
Safety First   92
At Your Service—What Dating Bureaus Offer   93

6. Stepping Out   96
Pull Yourself Together, Charlie Brown   97
If Nobody Goes to Singles Bars, How Come
    They're Always Full?   101
Being There—A Firsthand View of Singles Bars   108
Mix, Match, and Party Places   114
Stepping Out, Without Getting Stepped On:
    Rules for Success   116

7. Private Strategies

119

Public vs. Private—The Horror of Letting It All
Hang Out | 119
See You at the Veggies | 123
Truth and Consequences | 125
Airing Your Dirty Laundry | 126
Private Strategies Go Public—A Double-Edged
Sword | 129
The Energy Factor—Showing Your Peacock
Feathers | 130
Why Women Look and Men Don't | 134

8. Nothing Works Like Success

137

The Strategists | 137
The Joiners | 139
The Advertisers | 143
In the Neighborhood | 145
I'll See You at the Office | 147
Thinking Positive | 149
Know Thyself—The Fundamental Chord | 152
Summing Up—Points for Pondering | 154

9. A Look into the Future

157

Factor One—It Can't Last Forever | 157
Factor Two—His and Hers | 158
Factor Three—Knowing Your Options | 159
The Psychology of Change | 159
Changes and Readjustments | 162
Meeting—You're on Your Own | 166
Dating—The All-American Pastime | 168
TV Tribalism—The New Teachers | 170
Trends—Sketching Out Tomorrow | 173
Living Without You | 173
You're Not Getting Older . . . | 174
Summing Up | 176

Epilogue

178

Acknowledgments

We would like to thank Bess L. Silverman for her invaluable assistance in compiling supporting material for our book; Arlene Rossen Cardozo, for her sharp editorial comments, which helped us more clearly define the book in the early stages of its development; and Dan Lacy and Richard Levine for their wisdom about how to put our best foot forward in the publishing world.

We would also like to thank our respective husbands, Charles Kielkopf and Don Kumka, for their support, patience, and feedback throughout what seemed like a never-ending process of thinking, writing, and rewriting.

Last but not least, we would like to thank all the single men and women who shared their private thoughts and feelings with us and without whom there would be no book.

Introduction

This book began when Dr. O'Connor was teaching a university course in sex, romance, and relationships, and Dr. Silverman was interviewing newly married couples on issues of intimacy. Over casual lunches, we began applying our expertise to the local romantic scene. Graduate students are notorious for pursuing a degree with one mate and finishing it with another. But most interesting to us was the fact that no matter how terrible a past relationship had been, people were ardently seeking a replacement. Finding someone was a top priority, yet it apparently was not an easy task. Both men and women complained about how hard it was to meet someone. We overheard the same issue discussed in supermarket lines, while strolling in the park, and in busy theater lobbies. It became an intriguing puzzle; if both men and women were saying the same thing, what was preventing them from finding each other?

We decided to take on the challenge and put our sociological training to work. First we mapped out how we would attack the problem in a systematic and thorough way. Then we jumped in headfirst:

WANTED: Males and females, ages 25–60, single or divorced. We seek volunteers to participate in a research study designed to discover why so many people have such difficulty finding the right relationships. Join a small group discussion, about 2 hours, call 555-3232.

When we first ran this ad in the "eligibles" column of a large urban newspaper, we were completely unprepared for the overwhelming response. Not only did the phone ring off the hook with eager volunteers, but some people even lied about their age to get into a group! It seemed that every unattached male and female we talked with said they were totally preoccupied with finding a serious, committed relationship.

Was this simply a local phenomenon, or was it more widespread? The study began to grow from focus groups to in-depth interviews, to regional comparisons, to interviews with dating service directors, to historical analyses of popular magazines. We began interviewing men and women from all over the country, from all walks of life. Everywhere it was the same—New York, Los Angeles, Boston, Chicago, even Smalltown, U.S.A.—Everyone told us they wanted to meet someone special but that they couldn't find anyone.

There certainly has been no shortage of media attention to the problem of single men and women meeting one another. We've heard about it on "Donahue" and "Oprah" and read about it in such diverse publications as *U.S. News and World Report, Money Magazine, Cosmopolitan, Newsweek, Ms.,* and the *New York Times Magazine.* But despite the ready availability of facts about singles, no one has really presented the underlying problem: Society has changed in a way that no longer responds to the essential human need for intimacy.

Throughout our interviews we came to recognize that social attitudes had caused single people to believe that there was something essentially wrong with them because of their inability to establish relationships. We began to feel even more compelled to set the record straight—to show what happens when meeting someone has, for the first time, moved from the institutions of family, school, and church, and become the responsibility of the individual.

The future for singles is forever changed. We have entered a new era in which it is crucial that singles understand that they are not somehow deficient as human beings, but that the world in which they live has changed tremendously. To be successful in that world requires a map of the terrain. We sincerely hope this book will be your map.

Finding Love

1

When Institutions Fail

*F*rom the first cave date to the first tent marriage, men and women have plotted out the strategies of getting together. Whether it was a stroll along the Nile, or a candlelight dinner, there have been prescribed behaviors—the accepted and the expected, the right way and the wrong.

In the United States, until recently, the process of dating and mating was familiar and predictable. Family, school, and church were the accepted matchmakers of the day, but this is no longer true. Today most singles are over twenty-five, out of the school system, no longer living with their parents, and seldom in church. In a few short decades the world of meeting and dating has been turned upside down. Geographic mobility, delayed marriage, and rampant divorce rates have destroyed the relatively stable community of the presixties. The problem is that the main actors are totally unaware that the stage has collapsed.

Thirty years ago most singles remained in the protective custody of their families until they were ushered into the state of matrimony sometime in their early twenties. Choosing within a narrow geographic area and from a relatively small pool of eligibles, they managed to find each other, fall in love, and marry. But today, with unlimited geographic mobility and a seemingly endless variety of people from which to choose, the number-one complaint among singles is that they can't find anyone! Why is this so?

First of all, the very geographic mobility that appears to increase the pool of eligibles effectively shrinks it. Frequent job relocations cause people to move across the country before they've scarcely finished nodding their heads to the new

3

job, the big promotion, or the technological "gold rush." They wind up in New York, Chicago, or L.A. with their Cuisinarts tucked under their arms, strolling down streets filled with people who do not know their names. Often these displaced singles are not even aware they have left valuable networks behind, since they were not conscious of constructing them in the first place. Singles over thirty have the additional problem of shrinking networks as their friends begin to marry.

For the millions of divorced who reenter the ranks of the single, networks may remain, but they are the wrong ones. These singles find themselves linked to married friends, whose other friends are mostly married. Also, since the pool of "singles by divorce" is constantly changing through new entries and exits (i.e., divorce and remarriage), it is more difficult for this group to construct reliable networks.

Even the seemingly "endless variety" of people from which to choose can, ironically, make it harder to find someone. In the presixties world, singles were fairly homogeneous. If you were single, you were probably under thirty (more often under twenty-five), and looking for a lifelong mate. Today, being single may mean anything from "over thirty, never married," to "twice divorced and still looking." The diversity of race, social class, and personal history in any large metropolitan area can often make it harder to find the specific type of person you are looking for.

After interviewing hundreds of singles around the country, it became clear that the issue of meeting and dating was far more complex than could be addressed with a single solution. Your age, history, and present circumstances place you in a particular category. Josh, Madeline, and Clay each occupy a different place in the dating structure, which presents each of them with a distinct set of problems.

Single and Looking

Josh, a twenty-eight-year-old architect, was bright, good-looking, and more single than he had ever wanted to be. He

confided that he was afraid there was something very wrong with him. He never used to have a problem finding girl-friends. When he lived in Denver, he had never spent more than a few weeks between dating relationships. But from the time he moved to Chicago several years ago, things had been different—and he still could not figure out what had gone wrong.

It quickly became apparent that several things had indeed "gone wrong." In Denver Josh had been part of a large friendship network. Since he had grown up in that city, he had numerous social connections, so his transition from college to "the outside," was scarcely noticed. When he wanted a night out, all he needed to do was to pick up the phone and call his current girlfriend. Or if he was between girl-friends he would go to a friend's party, or a friend of a friend's party, to meet people. "There were so many of us who were basically unattached, men and women. We were all having a great time. Sometimes it was with someone special, and sometimes we were all just friends having fun. But it sure isn't like that now. Somewhere along the way I must have lost my touch."

It wasn't his "touch" Josh had lost, but his location. When he moved to Chicago, he severed his ties with an effective friendship network. His work as a consultant took him from one small firm to another; he was seldom in one job setting for more than three months. We asked him to think about these places and tell us how many single women he had met there who were in his general age range, who had similar values, and whom he also found somewhat attractive. He looked stunned. We never got to "attractive." Josh had not worked with even one woman who was unmarried and near his own age! The conclusion was so obvious, he laughed. The look of relief on his face was that of a man reprieved. All this time he had thought it was his own fault—that there was something wrong with him. Yet the explanation was so simple: If you don't meet, you don't date. He could hardly wait to get home and tell his room-

mate. "You should meet him," he told us. "He's good-looking, has a great job ... and would you believe we sit around on Saturday nights wondering what two guys like us are doing sitting at home alone on the weekend?"

Although institutional failure and other structural issues are the underlying cause of problems in meeting and dating, singles seem to be totally unaware of this fact. Instead they complicate the problem by blaming themselves for what they are quick to define as personal failure. In the course of the evening, Josh had mentioned something that had been bothering him for a long time. The year before, he had finally managed to meet a girl whom he found attractive and "very nice." They had a few dates that were mutually enjoyable, but Lynn was only on vacation, visiting friends, and at the end of the week she returned to L.A. Josh could not get her out of his mind. He called her a few times and then, deciding she was the girl for him, took some time off and flew to L.A. to spend a few days with her. It was a disaster. It turned out she had a steady boyfriend, had assumed Josh was coming to see her simply as a friend, and was horrified that there could have been such a misunderstanding. Josh flew back to Chicago chastened and demoralized. "It still bothers me when I think about it. It wasn't really Lynn. I made it into something that wasn't there because I needed someone so much. I don't even know if she was right for me ... she was okay ... but that's how desperate I was. I've seen other people like that. It's always a turnoff. I never thought I would act that way. That's for losers ... I've never thought of myself as a loser before."

This was a theme we heard over and over again, and found intriguing. Why does the notion of needing someone, of harboring that powerful, human drive for intimacy, instantly turn an otherwise successful, well-adjusted person into a loser? More important, in the context of meeting/dating, what *is* a "loser"? Gradually it became clear that "losing" is composed of two separate issues that become dangerously entwined. First, you win or lose depending on

how successfully you carry out the objective of meeting someone. If you are unable to meet someone, you have indeed "failed" in a specific behavior. But secondly, and more important, is the runoff: the tendency to expand the definition from an *activity* that has failed, to a *person* who has failed. The failed person becomes a "loser." It is a tidy, if sadly inaccurate little package. Why are we so quick to point the finger of blame at ourselves?

For one thing, self-reliance, autonomy, and individualism are deeply entrenched values for most of us. We've been raised with a general "when the going gets tough, the tough get going" mentality. If you can't solve your problems, it's your own fault. In the fifties and sixties, when family, church, and school were still functioning as matchmakers, the individual was free to concentrate on personal improvement or the charm factor. There were plenty of eligible people around; the goal was to attract the *most* eligible. Today, unfortunately, although the structure has changed, the advice has not.

Pick up any book or magazine on finding someone, and you see immediately that you are either too fat or too thin, too quiet or too gregarious, your clothes are too colorful or too dull, your hair is all wrong. Why should you believe all this criticism? Because if it wasn't true, you would have found someone by now. The Catch-22 of this mentality is that no matter what self-improvements you labor over, if they don't put a person on your doorstep, it's still your fault. You must have lost too much weight, built up too much muscle, or become too gregarious. Back to the drawing board.

Although there is nothing wrong with self-improvement advice, as a solution to finding an intimate relationship it is misleading. Telling people how to attract someone without addressing the underlying problem of how to *meet* someone is like equipping an expedition for deep-sea fishing in the desert.

Human beings need explanations. We give ourselves answers to make sense out of our world, learn from our mistakes, and hang on to some sense of control over our lives. Today the explanations aren't working. They aren't working because they fit an old model. The world of men and women meeting and dating has changed dramatically. But men and women are still operating under the old expectations, which means their understanding of what is happening, and their judgments of it, are inaccurate.

The Second Time Around

For the divorced, there are additional problems in meeting and dating. Madeline, a petite thirty-six-year-old mother of two, manages a small art gallery. She is pretty, vivacious, and has been divorced for nearly three years. Madeline complains that it is almost impossible to find eligible men. According to her, "It was nearly a year before I was willing to try dating again, and when I did, I found it's a pretty grim scene. The guys I've met are either married, mothered, or recovering from divorce. The nice ones have too many kids, are paying too much alimony, or found someone last week."

When Madeline married for the first time, she was twenty-six. Meeting men was not an issue for her. Most of the people she knew then were eligible, that is, single, never married, and probably looking for someone. There were lots of people around with the same goals: starting a career, finishing an education, finding a mate. Beyond that the goals were less clear, but there was the expectation of a standard format. Once married you would stroll down life's pathway with a certain amount of predictability and permanence. Madeline recalls feeling a mild sense of relief when she and Kevin were married. "It wasn't anything big, but it was definitely there... the feeling of clearing one more hurdle, of having your life solidly on course. Let's face it, that's one of the major tasks, choosing a partner, and we all assume it's for the rest of our lives. After all, why would you bother marrying someone if you thought it was a temporary arrangement? The statistics don't mean a thing. Divorce always happens to someone else."

After her divorce, Madeline was totally unprepared for the changes in the dating scene. "It was fun being single the first time around. I was friendly and social; men were comfortable with me. But it's so different now. When you're divorced you feel like a walking apology. Then there's the problem of kids. I love my two boys—they're terrific and I'm proud of them. But when you first meet someone, you can feel that is definitely a sorting factor. You're telling someone you come with extra baggage. It makes a difference for both the long-term and the short-term. Long-term could involve a ready-made family; for the short-term, baby-sitters get expensive and you can forget about the 'quiet dinner at my place' routine. If Jeffrey doesn't get you Jonathan will."

Although Madeline does bring an additional set of conditions to the dating arena, the problem is not the kids, and it's not the divorce. The problem is that she has passed beyond the "critical mass" stage for finding someone. If she is able to meet enough single men, she will not only find one who is both attracted and attractive to her, but also one who is looking for a family that includes an artistic mother and her small sons. The question is, since most of the people over thirty are no longer single, how does she meet those who are?

Madeline tried the same strategies at thirty-four that she had used so successfully at twenty-six, but with very different results. Even though she had lived in the same city for most of her life and knew lots of people, her formerly single friends were now married and no longer had a list of other singles. When Madeline asked her friends to introduce her to eligible men, they just didn't seem to know any. Their efforts to be helpful became the "if he's single, he's for Madeline" strategy. For Madeline the whole experience was demoralizing. "It makes you wonder about your friends. My major in college was art history—I'm an artist myself. The last man they introduced me to was a taxidermist who spends his vacations deer hunting."

The situation is no less harrowing for divorced males whose friends are also very married, but there are some differences. For one thing, since kids still tend to stay with Mom, a divorced man's home life is usually child-free. In addition, research shows that the standard of living for males tends to go up after divorce. Does this mean they are the free and gleeful playboys of the penthouse world? Far from it. Not only do divorced men also find that their friends are mostly married, but in addition it is their friends' wives who are in charge of the social calendar. This means, in effect, that these men are at the mercy of friends "once removed" when it comes to meeting someone. Clay, a forty-four-year-old divorced engineer, recalls a series of blind dates that had been arranged for him by the wife of a friend. "She worked at a welfare agency, and every time some woman came in with a couple of kids and no husband, she would invite me over for dinner. Then one of these women would show up. It didn't matter if they hadn't finished high school, or that we didn't have anything in common. I was single, so I would probably be interested. Finally I just stopped accepting her invitations."

Although Clay would eventually like to remarry, he does not see many alternatives for finding someone. As an engineer, he works mostly with other men and has little opportunity for meeting women as part of his daily routine. The fact that his wife had been in charge of their social life means he has few personal contacts that are his own. Added to this is what he described as the "being out of practice" factor. "There have been a couple of parties—the Christmas party at work, that sort of thing—but I'm not used to going to those things alone. I'm not very good at starting a conversation. I usually stand around by myself, and after a while I leave."

An additional hurdle for divorced people entering the meeting/dating scene is simply, as Clay observed, being out of practice. Most of us tend to forget that social skills, like any others, atrophy without use. So what do you do? The first step, of course, is getting back into practice. Without a willingness to experience the initial awkwardness of first parties, first meetings, and first dates, you never will feel comfortable with them.

But most important is the issue of how to meet someone in the first place. What do you do if you are divorced today and looking? For one thing, you need to be aware that the structure as you have known it, and your place in that structure, is changed. No more college classrooms and football games with dozens of potential partners within easy flirting distance; no more friends to "fix you up." Relying on your married friends to find you someone is a little like trying to borrow money from a bag lady; they can't give you what they don't have.

Finding Someone—The Demographic Dilemma

Today if you want to find someone, it really is your responsibility—along with about fifty million other singles. Not only are there plenty of other singles around, but the record number of divorces in the United States today means there is a large, *constantly changing* pool of singles wanting to meet and date. If you don't find someone, there probably isn't anything wrong with *you*, but there probably *is* something wrong with your strategy.

In the midst of all of this, the key thing to remember is not only that structure is of prime importance, but that your *place* in the structure is equally important. The view from Lady Liberty is quite different depending on whether you're standing at the top of the torch or on the big toe. The structural factors that affect your meeting/dating life are not the same for each individual or group. Structure has to be scrutinized by first looking at the specific place in which you fit, and then understanding those factors that directly impact on your territory. The situation is not the same for the unmarried twenty-seven-year-old as it is for the divorced thirty-five-year-old, and it is different for the never-married forty-year-old and for the divorced fifty-year-old. But the first step in solving the problem of meeting someone is the same for everyone, that is, to understand the nature of the problem itself.

The "rock and the hard place" of the dating world is the choice between believing that the inability to find someone is entirely your own fault, which sets you up for massive personal failure, or believing that, because of demographics and the male-to-female ratio, the whole thing is preordained—a matter of luck anyway, so why bother trying? Especially if you're female. One look at the numbers will seal your doom. After all, numbers never lie—or do they?

Picture Jackie, twenty-nine, relaxing over a leisurely cup of coffee on a typical, bright, Sunday morning. She picks up the *Times* and reads another eye-catching article about the plight of singles in urban America. The bad news is directed at her and she reads it with undeviating focus. The plain fact seems to be that there simply are not enough unattached men to go around. Place yourself in the appropriate age category and the facts become even more explicit: if you are between twenty-five and twenty-nine there are 7.7 men for every 10 women; between thirty-five and thirty-nine there are 4.8 men for every 10 women; and between forty-five and forty-nine there are only 3.8 men for every 10 women. Jackie conjures up visions of parties and special gatherings with fewer and fewer men and more and more women trying ever harder to win the coveted prize. Although it's not a rosy picture, Jackie is thankful for her relative youth—at least the percentages are more favorable in her age category. She reads on. Two professors at Yale and Harvard have just completed a study on white, college-educated women. According to their findings, if these women have not married by the time they reach thirty, they have only a 20 percent chance of ever doing so. Jackie calculates on her fingers; she has seven months left. With a sigh, she tosses the paper aside—another Sunday ruined.

On the Upper West Side, David, a thirty-four-year-old marketing analyst, is reading the same article. Puzzled, he puts down the paper; it does not ring true. Everything he's reading suggests that he and his bachelor friends should be having the time of their lives. According to this, all of these women should be practically coming out of the woodwork. But that's just not the way it is. He and his friends spend far too much time sitting at home by themselves, going to some sporting event together, or going out for a drink at one of the singles bars. It's true there are always plenty of women in the bars, but they aren't the kind of women he is looking for. He used to hope that someone really special would just happen to come in the bar that one time; perhaps her friend would persuade her to stop, and then he would meet her....

So what's wrong with this picture? Why hasn't David met one of the Jackies around? And what about Jackie? Should she fold her cards and go home? Before jumping to any conclusions, the numbers need to be examined more carefully.

A new study conducted by the U.S. Census Bureau provides us with a strikingly different picture of the situation. For example, Jackie, who is now thirty and still recovering from the trauma of the Yale–Harvard study, would be ecstatic to know that her chances of getting married have just increased by over 300 percent! This new study reports that by age thirty, single, white, college-educated women have a 66 percent chance of marrying, by age thirty-five a 41 percent chance, and by age forty, almost one in four women will eventually marry. What happened during the time between these two reports? Can a study bearing the Yale–Harvard name be that far off the mark? The answer is yes—for a variety of reasons, some statistical and some sociological. The more you understand about such studies the more you are able to see their limitations and understand why you can't simply apply the data to your life situation.

Rather than looking into a crystal ball, researchers use historical and current data about marital behavior to make predictions about the future. Interpretations and assumptions are made about this information and then it is translated into mathematical formulas and tested on a sample of people. Different results are not uncommon.

Let's say you were an avid fan of horse racing. You would read up on the past performance of the horse, the jockey, and the trainer. Then you would mentally place these facts into your formula for picking a winner. Your formula might give extra importance to the jockey, whereas someone else's might put more weight on how fast the horse ran its last three races. The bottom line is that you are likely to give this horse a different chance of winning than the next person.

The same thing happened with the Yale–Harvard and Census Bureau researchers. By paying attention to different facts, they came up with different predictions about your chances of getting married. The most important point to remember is that these are just hypothetical models of how things might turn out for the mythical average person. They don't predict anything about you as a unique individual.

An interesting statistic that is constantly appearing in the media is the male/female ratio. This would appear to be a simple task—mere headcounting—but in fact, there are many ways to produce this ratio; and like the Yale–Harvard and Census Bureau studies, each is based upon different assumptions about human behavior, past and present. The critical assumption in figuring out this ratio is the age difference between men and women who marry. For example, you don't want to compare the number of single women aged thirty to thirty-three to the number of single men of the same age, because most women choose their mate from an older pool of men. But what is appropriate? Is it better to compare these women to the number of men aged thirty-two to thirty-five? Thirty-three to thirty-six? How about thirty to forty? The results from one comparison could send you packing for the nearest Club Med while those from another might spell RELIEF from the ongoing search for a mate.

Apart from these more technical issues, there are even more basic problems with the numbers that are reported. For one thing, eligible men are not evenly distributed around the country, as women in Buffalo or Washington, D.C., know only too well. Second, although the numbers in Phoenix may look great for husband hunting, and Boston, numerically, may sound like a bachelor's delight, before you pack your bags, consider this: Numbers mean nothing by themselves; it is the interpretation that counts. An old vaudeville joke goes, "Did you know that somewhere in the world today a woman gives birth every minute?" Response: "Good heavens! Somebody better find that woman and stop her."

The Numbers Game—New Light on an Old Problem

Most singles statistics are the result of dredging through the U.S. Bureau of the Census data, which compiles its findings in numerous forms. It is up to social scientists to coax meaningful information out of the many categories. In the process, numbers sometimes lose their quantitative precision and become ephemeral. For example, one of the reasons women like Jackie are quoted such poor odds for finding a mate is because of a phenomenon known as "the marriage gradient." The two prongs of the marriage gradient are age and social status. In terms of sheer numbers, age works more favorably for men, since they tend to marry women their own age or younger. For women, the trend has been to marry men the same age or older, leaving them with a much smaller pool of eligibles. The fifty-year-old male can generally consider choosing a mate from a pool of women anywhere from near thirty to near fifty. The fifty-year-old woman, on the other hand, more typically has chosen from men who are fifty and over. This means she not only has fewer people to choose from than her male counterpart, but her competition includes the pool of younger women as well.

The second part of the marriage gradient, social status, is the notion of "marrying up" or "marrying down." College-educated women rarely become involved with men who are less educated than they are; as a result, for women with increasing education, the pool of eligible men begins to shrink. The better a woman's job, or the higher her income, the more difficult it will be for her to find a man with equal or better resources. However, as men become more educated, it is a different story. Since men typically choose mates who are *at or below* their own status level, for them, more education or a better job only increases the pool of eligible women. What then is the solution for the successful woman: to quit her job and lie about her degrees? According to the statistics, won't that increase her pool of eligibles?

Definitely not. For one thing, just because women tended to marry up in the past, does not mean that they will continue to do so. When men were generally the only wage earners in a family, it made good sense for women to be very careful about the occupation and education of their future husbands. Now, with the trend toward both partners working, the future of the family unit is not as critically tied to the woman's marital choice, so she need not be as restricted.

Also, the issue of age needs to be reexamined. There is no reason to assume that the pattern of women choosing partners who are older or the same age will continue. Although we are just beginning to see evidence of women marrying younger men in greater numbers, there is good reason to expect this to increase. Why? Exchange theory applied to choice of marriage partners basically looks at what each has to bargain with for the "best deal." Traditionally the woman's youth and beauty has been weighed in the pot against the man's potential as a breadwinner. However, as more and more women are beginning to earn the bread themselves, they can bargain in the same arena. The result will most likely be that in the future we shall see an increase of educated women with good occupations choosing mates from among younger men.

Lastly, before letting numbers do the fortune-telling for your meeting/dating future, consider the most basic issue of all. Whether there are ten men for every five women or five men for every ten women does not matter one bit if you don't have a way to meet each other. Numbers represent nothing more than potential. Let's face it, David probably sweeps past several hundred single women every day—in elevators, on the subway, at restaurants, in his office building—but he doesn't really *meet* any of them. It is the same for Jackie. There may be more single women in New York than single men, but the fact is, in sheer numbers, there are still *plenty* of single men.

If you are female, the issue is how to make sure that in your statistical group of 10 women, you wind up with one of the 7.7 or 4.8 men available. Someone is meeting and dating these men; it may as well be you.

If you are male, the issue may be primarily how to make sure you *meet* the single women who are around. A friend recently described her forty-year-old cousin's wedding: "He looked so happy, I couldn't resist asking him what everyone in the family wondered. Why did he stay a bachelor for so long? Do you know what he said? 'I was never a bachelor—I just couldn't find anyone until now.' "

2

We Touched a Nerve

Dr. O'Connor's university course on intimacy and human sexuality never failed to fill quickly. During spring quarter there were always a few couples taking it prior to their June wedding. Not surprisingly, the classroom mood was frequently romantic, flirtatious, and exciting. Instead of studying "Sociology of Law" or "Problems of Hunger in World Populations," these men and women were studying about the chemistry that makes the world go round—love. As an added bonus, they were getting class credit for investigating a topic that occupied so much of their free time anyway.

When we look back at the classroom surveys they were asked to fill out on dating and partner selection, it is clear that these students, whether single, engaged, or "involved," were indeed the innocents. Their definitions of love frequently sounded like throwaway lines from the top ten hits: "Love is the most wonderful thing in the world." "Love is sharing the good times and the bad." "Love is like floating on air."

Comparing student surveys to the comments on love and dating made by those over twenty-five with whom we did in-depth interviews was like comparing a Disney cartoon to a Bergman film. Comments from the older group tended to be more practical, less effusive, and sometimes hostile: "Love is a solid gold Cadillac." "Love is when you can get up in the morning and go all day without a fight." "Love sucks."

These were the veterans—all too many of them cynical, battle-scarred, and emotionally battered. We wanted to know, in part, what happens between the time of easy friendships of men and women on campus and in the classroom, and the time when dating is treated with the same anticipation as life in a war zone. Although it may not be plunder and pillage, according to singles themselves the current dating scene all too often comes uncomfortably close. Why?

To better understand the current male/female dynamics, we set up focus group interviews where men and women, in similar age ranges, talked about their experiences in today's dating climate. For this segment of our research we placed an ad in the eligibles column of a large urban newspaper, requesting volunteers. The response was overwhelming. Something serious, even threatening, was going on, and people were anxious to talk about it.

From the Sound of Many Voices

We listened to hundreds of single men and women throughout the United States, both in focused group interviews with men and women together, and in individual in-depth interviews. The obvious is that times have changed; what is not so obvious is the extent to which these changes have caused social upheaval.

Single men and women no longer know what to expect from each other in the major areas of love, career, money, and sex—not necessarily in that order. Shifting values based on changing times, a lack of clear social expectations, and the absence of role models have made singles wary. For many, the natural excitement and sense of adventure connected with dating at younger ages has turned into the grim pursuit of avoiding another Saturday night alone.

In discussions with both men and women, their comments, complaints, and insights revealed several key issues where broad social change has led to complex problems mistakenly interpreted by individuals as personal shortcomings.

The Rise of the "Me" Generation

The values that inspired Madison Avenue to label an entire group as the "me" generation do not exist in a vacuum.

It is to be expected that the children of an affluent society will be affected by its goals. Although human nature does not change over time, socially imbedded expectations do. Asked to describe those expectations, the responses were strikingly similar.

"I wouldn't want to give up my individuality. I'm independent; I don't want to worry about someone else. I don't understand how anyone could give themselves up completely to a relationship" (thirty-six-year-old female).

"I'm reasonably happy with my life, but sometimes I think that that in itself keeps me from a relationship. I don't want someone to come in and try to change the way I live" (thirty-two-year-old male).

"I'm glad to see women in the work force sharing equal slices of the pie. But I wish they would be more equal than that—that they would take more responsibility in relationships instead of expecting men to do it all" (forty-one-year-old male).

"I think men like the liberated woman more than the traditional. She's more stimulating to talk to, even if she's more threatening. They're proud of women with professional careers. It's important to them. But they also want someone sweet and not too bitchy—not too demanding. They want it all" (twenty-seven-year-old female).

A major theme underlying these interviews is the thinly disguised view men and women today have of each other as adversaries; players on opposing teams. We do not deny that there has always been a difference between the sexes in goals connected with dating and courtship. The caveat of my Irish grandmother, delivered periodically to the women of the family, no doubt exists in some version in every language under the sun: "Before they get you they give you chocolates, and when they get you they give you nothing."

But today there is a major difference in attitude. Both males and females have moved from benign acceptance of the foibles and shortcomings of the opposite sex to a stern appraisal of their deficits.

The Price of Cupid's Arrow—Cost vs. Reward

Recent years have witnessed the growing popularity of exchange theory applied to relationships. Based on an economic model, exchange theory in its simplest form says that individuals will always act to gain the greatest rewards for the least costs. In a relationship this means getting the best deal you can—expending the least effort for the most payback. We all have some subliminal awareness of this. You see a gorgeous twenty-two-year-old woman with a paunchy man of sixty, and your first thought is, "He must have money." Exchange routinely operates in the tendency people have to marry those from similar social backgrounds and educational levels. If they want to "marry up," they need additional bargaining power in the form of personal or social assets.

Although there is nothing essentially wrong with exchange theory, it becomes problematic when an attempt is made to transform everything into units of specific value. How do you weigh her M.A. in accounting against his Ph.D. in romance languages? Or an additional $5,000 a year in salary against a congenial personality? Is a million-dollar smile really worth it? One of the problems in assigning cost/reward value is that factors without an easy price tag often get left out of the equation altogether. Those essential human characteristics get little attention in a competitive market where we have been exhorted to get the most for least.

A thirty-eight-year-old computer salesman summed it up this way: "Look, everyone wants to get all they can for themselves; that's the way it's always been. It's just that today there's more to be gotten."

A thirty-four-year-old woman specializing in new products research told us, "I'm not embarrassed by wanting the best. It shows that I know how to tell the difference. Hey, if I can get perfection, I'll take it."

A twenty-nine-year-old chemist explained the source of

his goals: "I grew up in a lower-middle-class family—old cars, houses that always needed fixing. Why would I want that? My brother is five years older, has his own condo, travels, dresses great; that's my role model."

While the phenomenon of dating is not new, the principal actors are the products of a new age. The trend toward increased independence, implicit in the "take charge" attitude of the eighties, has promoted an increase in individual self-interest. For those who are dating, it has created a new set of problems and demands, which have in turn given rise to rapidly changing personal expectations and behaviors.

Mark is thirty-seven, good-looking, never married. A product engineer with a bright future, he is obsessed with finding the perfect match—a woman who will be his intellectual, financial, and moral equal. He applies the same principles he uses in business to his search for the ideal mate. According to him, "I haven't got time to waste. You've got to know what you want and go for it." He told us about one incident where he had met a woman through a mutual friend. "When I picked her up for our first date, we drove for about a block and she said something that offended me; some women's lib thing. I turned the car around, drove her back to her apartment and told her to get out. She was one surprised lady. But I don't take crap. I know what I want and what I don't."

At the time we interviewed Mark, he seemed genuinely puzzled about the problems he was having finding women to date. He complained, "I think women are generally unpredictable. They seem to expect you to do everything for them. I've just about given up on dating."

Kate, a twenty-nine-year-old Phi Beta Kappa currently working as a lobbyist in Washington, complained, "Too many people call it quits before giving the person a chance. They have all become so individually oriented—they look out for number one. They're so self-centered. They demand perfection. If someone doesn't live up to their expectations, they will just look for someone else."

Kate recently ended a long-distance relationship with a Boston attorney. Michael's first marriage lasted scarcely two years and ended in divorce. The reason he gave was vague; they "just weren't right for each other." Kate thought she and Michael were the perfect couple, and had prepared expectantly for her last weekend in Boston. But instead of the anticipated proposal, Michael became furious when she suggested the wallpaper he chose for his apartment was too dark. "He decided I was too critical, that we were too different, and that we shouldn't see each other anymore. That was it. No second chance. I know I'm better off without someone like that, but I really cared about him. We could have worked it out."

A major stumbling block for the "me" generation is the demand for the perfect relationship, delivered with the speed of a midnight pizza. Instead of learning to put more effort into each succeeding relationship, men and women often use a failure to confirm their suspicions that they may be one of the few perfect people left in the world.

Great Expectations

Changing expectations have also meant a new look at the old question of occupation. Traditionally women have been expected to seek men with a higher level of occupation than their own, to provide for themselves and their children. This has been part of the marrying-up phenomenon. Men, on the other hand, have traditionally paid little attention to the occupation of their potential partner, since they expected to be the primary source of family income. But this too has undergone significant change. Some of the most successful men interviewed insisted their partners have close to the same educational level and salary potential as themselves.

Peter, a forty-year-old city planner, is firm in his expectations. "I don't need a woman to make as much as I do, but I do expect her to have a profession and professional goals. With so many women in the labor force today, I guess I would feel cheated if I married someone who just wanted to stay home. I know guys that has happened to. They marry some good-looking waitress, or sales clerk, who decides to quit her job two weeks after the wedding, because it's boring. The poor guy is stuck."

Ben, a thirty-three-year-old internal auditor, says he never paid any attention to a woman's earnings until he entered the world of work himself. "Twelve years ago I was still a student. It didn't matter what a person did or where she was from. But as you get out in the world and support yourself, you see things differently. Money makes life easier." He now looks for someone as goal-oriented and achievement-oriented as himself.

According to Paul, a forty-one-year-old divorced airline pilot, "One of the best reasons for marrying a woman with a good job is the possibility of divorce. If you're realistic you have to think about that. If you marry someone and you're the sole source of support, what then? I know—it's cost me plenty. But I've learned something too. The first time I married for love; the second time it will be for money."

But money is not the only reason men are seeking women with similar professional goals. Thirty-four-year-old Kevin is vice-president of the family corporation and grew up wealthy. For him professional goals mean interest and enthusiasm. "It's all comparative. Bright women today are usually in some sort of profession. That may have been different thirty or forty years ago. But today if a woman isn't doing something interesting, she either doesn't have the brains or creativity it takes. I want someone with both."

Brian, a twenty-nine-year-old mathematician, doesn't discount earning power as an important aspect of a job, but he ranks it second. "To me, any woman who is satisfied to make ten or twelve thousand a year doesn't have a very high opinion of herself. I look at a woman's job more as an indication of what she thinks about herself and her future—except if the job is very altruistic. Some terrifically dedicated social workers make zilch, but that's okay."

Women with a Future

While men have been busy evaluating the professional worth of the women with whom they may become involved, successful women are demanding even more success from the male population, for a variety of reasons.

Katherine had acquired a reputation as a gifted computer programmer even before completing her engineering degree. By age thirty she had sold several programs outright and was collecting royalties on others. Now in her midthirties, she earns over $80,000 a year. Asked if her comfortable financial circumstances made dating easier, she was adamant. "Absolutely not. There are a lot of deadbeats around only too glad to cash in on someone else's hard work. I can hardly believe I said that, but it's true. A lot of guys who are single now have blown it one way or another. Either they've screwed up their marriage with alcohol or drugs, or they can't hold a steady job. Now I understand why men used to be so cautious about women going out with them just for their money.

"I dated one guy for eight months. Karl always invented these wonderfully romantic, inexpensive dates. All summer we went to outdoor concerts, long walks, Shakespeare in the park, picnics with white wine. At first it was great. I didn't know exactly what he did for a living except he was some kind of a sales rep and that his work was 'off again, on again.' I knew I made a lot more money than he did, and I used to get tickets for any of the expensive things we wanted to go to. Everything was fine until fall came and he wanted to move in. I was a little hesitant, but in the end went along with it. What a disaster! Karl never paid a dime for anything. He ate all the food, drank the liquor, never worked. I would come home and he would be on the phone, or lying around watching TV. The last straw was when he asked me if I would mind getting him a couple of new shirts. I thought, 'Oh my god, there's a name for men like that.' Needless to say, I threw him out. But it was a weird experience. Now I don't want to date anyone who doesn't make at least as much as I do."

For the successful woman, the unexpected but nagging concern is ever present: "Is it my charm or my paycheck?" This anxiety, new for most women, is complicated by the fact that women cannot look to a previous generation of high-earner female role models to serve as examples. These women are the first. They are not only winning the bread, but croissants as well, and paying a price for it.

"It's hard when everyone acts as though you must have it all together, so you probably don't want or need their input," says Leslie, a twenty-nine-year-old fashion designer. "My own mother always says something like, 'Well, Leslie, I know whatever it is you'll work it out. You always have.' Everyone assumes just because you're competent in your job, everything else follows. Since I work in a glamour business people assume I have more dates than I can handle. No way. Most of my jobs are for gorgeous women or gay men. And after a fifty- or sixty-hour workweek, I don't have a lot of time to go looking. Worse yet, whenever I do 'look,' I become more aware of the fact that every time my income goes up, the number of eligibles goes down."

Although some women were concerned about income to avoid feeling exploited, others were concerned that a higher salary than that of a potential partner would remove the possibility of ever leaving the work force. Wells, a thirty-three-year-old CPA, includes income as one of her top priorities in a long-term relationship. "I don't want to get serious about someone who makes less than I do. What if we wanted to marry and have a family? How could we afford it if I was making most of the money? Besides, I don't want to work forever—at least not full-time."

There is no doubt that the issue of making a living is a powerful one, for both men and women. But a number of women who have been in the labor market for a decade or more view men's new interest in female careers with a dim eye.

Marcia, a thirty-seven-year-old hair stylist, is convinced her dating life is affected by her income. According to her, "I think men are really looking for someone who is making a lot of money—someone to join forces with. Sometimes I don't think they view it as marriage as much as forming a corporation."

Jobless in Utopia

In a dating climate of "you show me your IRA and I'll show you mine," unemployment can be a social disaster as well as a financial one. Richard was between jobs when he returned to Minneapolis, tired of eight years as a part-time ski bum/instructor/bartender. His complaint was that he scarcely began a conversation with a woman before she asked him the inevitable, "So, what do you do for a living?" "When I said I was unemployed, I could see myself disappear before her. I no longer existed."

Richard told us when he first arrived in Minneapolis he had begun answering numerous personal ads "just to get some social life going. But it was the same thing on the phone. The first thing they asked me about was my job. When they heard I wasn't working, you could sense this choking little gasp on the other end of the line. They could barely finish the conversation. One woman was very up front. She said, 'Look, call me when you've got a job.' For most of them I don't think a 'job' was enough. I got the impression it had to be 'neurologist' or 'physicist'—or some other 'ist' with big bucks attached. I was talking to one woman who had already written me off. I said 'I suppose it would be different if I was an engineer or something.' She said 'God, not an engineer; half of them are always out of work.' I couldn't even pick the right imaginary job!"

Richard's experience was mirrored in the opinions of both men and women. There was little forgiveness for unemployment. If you didn't have a job, you searched until you found one. And the rule "never quit one job until you have signed the contract for another" is at least as ironclad today as in the past.

Jean, a thirty-year-old cost analyst, remarked, "A lot of people don't like their jobs, or think about moving on to something better. But you can't be irresponsible about it. I dated one guy a couple of times. He was 'temporarily' unemployed. He didn't have a car, so I had to pick him up, use my gas, pay parking, and because I felt sorry for him, go dutch. You can see why that didn't last."

As Jean's experience illustrates, avoidance of the unemployed is not necessarily based on snobbishness, but may be due to the very practical principle that "if there's no money to come out of your pocket, it will probably come out of mine."

On Your Best Behavior—Changing Norms

Although the tally is not yet in on the political effectiveness of the women's movement, there is no doubt that it has had an enormous effect on the way men and women relate to one another. Women have had ample opportunity to state their preferences and, according to some, "Men have bowed their heads, listened, and to the great dismay of women, totally misunderstood."

Ralph is a youthful forty-three, owns a travel agency, and generally thinks of himself as congenial and self-assured. But he confesses, "I have a problem figuring out what I'm supposed to do these days. Women are much more aggressive now. Fifteen years ago they wouldn't ask a man out—at least that's my experience. Now they have a whole agenda about what is right and wrong on a date—whether you pay or not. If you pay, you insult them; if you don't, you're tight. I don't even know who's supposed to pay for the cab anymore. Men were confused before, but no one was dumping on them to make them more confused. I dated one woman who kept telling me how important it was to talk about feelings, and how much she really cared for sensitive men.

We were having dinner at her place one night, and I told her about an incident that I had found really embarrassing. Boy, was that a mistake. I was expecting a little sympathy. Instead she looked at me like I had two heads."

Women find the situation equally frustrating. A twenty-eight-year-old photographer complained, "When we talk, he says he knows what I mean, but when it comes to doing something, he's always a little oblique. Then he says, 'Tell me, what did I do now?' How do you explain?"

The issue of male sensitivity, or lack of it, has been a source of confusion for both sexes. Often there is a basic lack of understanding about the definition. One woman voiced the opinion of many when she told us, "Too many guys confuse sensitivity with using you as a garbage dump. I don't trust someone who spills his guts the first time I'm out with him—or any time early on. It's creating demands. A really sensitive person would never do that."

Barbara, a thirty-one-year-old English instructor at a small eastern college, remarked, "I'm tired of listening to men's problems. I don't want to be someone's analyst. It makes me angry if I come back from a date and realize I've spent most of my time listening. So many of my relationships have been based on that—the fact that I'm such a good listener. I'm especially down on intellectuals. They're the worst."

The values of the "me" generation, with its emphasis on self-interest and maximizing profit, whether in love or finance, have had a differing impact on different age groups. In a "trickle up/trickle down" effect, everyone has been touched by changing social values. In the process a variety of new dating categories have emerged.

Once a Jerk...

One popular saying about men used to be "all the good ones are taken." In this age of easy divorce, they may have been taken, but on close examination, tossed back. The experience of the divorced man is far different from that of the long-term bachelor who has had ample opportunity to practice his social skills with continual dating. The divorced man, on the other hand, is all too often busy catching up on an arrested adolescence. He may look perfectly acceptable on the outside, but inside may be lurking what some women have described as one of the most irritating male categories —the second-generation jerk.

Laura, an assistant editor for a major fashion magazine, has dated frequently during the eight years since her college graduation. But according to her, the quality of eligible men is on a steady decline. "It's true. It's getting worse every year. Roger is a perfect example. He's forty-two, divorced for two years, a talented packaging designer, Princeton graduate, and a five-star jerk. Everything he does is to create an impression—finding the 'perfect little restaurant,' talking about all those exhausting New York parties. I've lived here for ten years. What does he think he's telling me? He drives a Porsche, has his dinner parties catered, and complains that alimony keeps him broke. He's like a little kid who's just been let out of the house, trying to do everything the big kids do. Even the way he talks; his conversation is a composite of *Playboy* and Julia Childs. If it's 'in,' he's seen it, done it, or has tickets. Any minute I'm waiting for him to say, 'Are we having fun yet?' The problem is, there's a whole group like that out there. Forget having a relationship with them. They're too busy catching up on all the fun they think they've missed."

A variation of this type was described by Sallie, a thirty-year-old medical researcher. "I didn't know Jack very well the first time he asked me out. He seemed very nice; a little too meticulous, maybe, like Felix in the 'Odd Couple.' He was thirty-eight, had a little girl, and had been divorced for about three years. At first I was very impressed. He really knows how to dress, was up on all the latest styles, knew all the little theaters and out-of-the-way galleries. But after a while I began to catch on. Everything was for show—he was the star of his own production. If I forgot for one minute to tell him how inventive or entertaining or clever he was, and what a great evening he'd planned, he'd start to pout.

"Once at a dinner party he was describing how he had been jogging one morning before work and, when he got back to his apartment to shower, discovered the water had been shut off for repairs. There wasn't a drop to be had, so guess what? He poured a whole case of Perrier into the tub, and had a *real* French bubble bath. Isn't that 'too cute'? What a creep."

The jerks of high school and college haven't changed; they're just packaged differently. Experience has taught them to tone down enough of the obviously obnoxious, to make them a little harder to identify, but they are still there. Why avoid them? Because the major feature of the jerk is not his superficial habits, but the self-centeredness that makes him oblivious to the needs and feelings of other people. The jerk of ten or twenty years ago may very likely be a well-paid professional who on the surface appears to be just like anyone else. He dresses appropriately, knows how to order the right wine, displays a superficial politeness. But underneath it all he is still a jerk, committed only to himself.

The Midas Syndrome

One of the most surprising aspects of the interviews, in general, was the frank emphasis on money, with a capital *M*. In the past, it was never considered "nice" to enter a relationship with dollar signs in both eyes instead of stars. Still, there was always a certain group who subscribed to the values portrayed in the now classic "Diamonds are a girl's best friend" and who agreed wholeheartedly with Mae West's proverbial response to the question of how she managed to keep her sex appeal over the years. She was purported to have answered in her throaty contralto, "Honey, when your looks go, you better have plenty of money; there's nothing sexier than that."

In a world where women have traditionally traded beauty and charm for male money and earning power, female concern with finances is not surprising. What was surprising to us as interviewers is the sudden frankness of that concern. To talk openly about money goals, especially when they involve the financial worth of your latest love, used to be far more taboo than sex ever was. It was a little like discussing issues of inheritance. Although most adults realize they will probably be heirs to their parents' estate, it would be in poor taste to show up at the hospital asking, "Mom, how much will we get when Dad dies?"

Yet in the world of romance, there has been a definite shift from "for richer or for poorer" to the prenuptial agreement. For those who are dating, the emphasis on money is cause for varying degrees of discomfort. No one wants to feel cheated, and yet mixing money and romance often smacks of something sleazy. Among those we interviewed, money ranked high as an important issue, but the reasons varied for men and women.

The Pay Date

Greg, forty-four, is an insurance broker who dates frequently. Like a growing number of males, he feels he has benefited from the feminist injunction that urges women to pay their own way, as a demonstration of their independence. According to him, "the 'equal pay' date is the best thing to come along since the zipper. I used to get tired of paying for everything. You look at the price of a show and multiply by two—that gets expensive. Besides, why shouldn't women pay? They're earning money, too."

Brent, a thirty-seven-year-old attorney, also feels strongly that women should pay. He still resents the fact that in addition to dividing the real estate, he had to continue support-

ing his former wife while she returned to school for professional training. "I paid for my education *before* we were
married. Why should I pay for hers, too? I used to be a very
generous guy. But when you're divorced, your opinions
change."

Although this reflects the popular view for many men,
others continue to feel uncomfortable expecting a woman to
pay her own way. "Call it macho if you want, I still feel
weird asking a woman out and then standing there while she
digs around in her purse."

At the same time, a number of men report they are uncertain what to do when the woman insists on paying. Most
agree it's better not to argue in those cases. As one man put
it, "I've always figured the date doesn't want to feel obli-
gated."

Among women, opinions are divided on whether or not to
pay your own way. Gina, a medical secretary and thirty-
eight-year-old mother of two, was adamant. "If I wanted to
be liberal, I'd be liberal—I don't want that. If he invites you
out, he should pay. The man is still the man. I like it that
way."

In sharp contrast, a thirty-six-year-old court reporter told
us, "Let's face it. Money is for buying. When I go out with
some guy I want to make sure he doesn't think he's made a
purchase. Besides, why should they have to pay all the time,
and pay your way too?"

Some women have found a middle ground. Greta, a tall,
athletic-looking fifty-five-year-old, told us, "I don't know
what the problem is. If you have a sense of fair play, you
never let things get to the point where you're wondering if
you should pay. Sometimes you pick up tickets for the symphony, or invite him for dinner, or plan a long walk and
coffee along the way. It doesn't need to be expensive."

Although Greta's solution may work well for long-term
relationships, several women pointed out there are many
dates where you do not see the same person more than once

or twice. In those cases, they argue, the price of casual dating can add up fast.

The argument runs both ways and across sexes. However, both men and women agree: It takes money to be single. And for many women, the extra money it takes to date often keeps them home. "The guys I go out with still make a lot more than I do. Besides, there are enough things I do have to pay for. When people talk about singles bars or singles clubs, those things aren't free."

Twenty-eight-year-old Rita is a nurse in the coronary care unit of a large city hospital. "I work hard and I don't make that much money. It's really unfair when men expect women to go fifty-fifty, dutch treat. They take unfair advantage of women's lib in that situation. It can be embarrassing. I've had a dinner date where the man makes a big thing out of dividing the bill, in front of other people, yet. That's really tacky. Or you stop for an ice cream cone and while you're finding a table, he goes to the counter to get his and leaves you to buy your own."

For women with children, money problems are compounded because even the simplest date involves an investment. Jeanette, a slim blonde with finely chiseled features, talked about the expense of hiring baby-sitters. "In the suburb where I live, none of the teenagers seem to need baby-sitting money. Everyone hires services, and they cost five dollars per hour. If I hired a sitter for Evan every time I wanted to go out, I would go broke. A man who offers to pay my sitter is certainly going to look better to me than one who thinks I should go dutch for dinner when I have a thirty-dollar sitter's fee waiting for me at home. Money does make a difference."

The Prenuptial Agreement—Yours, Mine, and Ours

In the past it was not unusual for men to be concerned about the disposition of assets in a long-term relationship.

However, with greater numbers of women accruing their own assets, the concern cuts both ways. Men and women who would willingly climb the highest mountain for each other pale at the mention of community property.

As one might expect, the economic aspects of marriage are of greatest concern to those who have assets to protect. Elizabeth, a thirty-four-year-old psychologist, is financially very well off, but she is quick to point out, "I did it all myself. I worked my way through college, paid off my loans, invested well, and saved hard. I'm not about to marry someone if it means risking everything I've worked for. I'm all for the prenuptial agreement."

Rhea, a twenty-six-year-old, auburn-haired model, presented another point of view. She told us, "I have very mixed feelings. For some people a prenuptial agreement is fine, but I also know I would never do it. It's too much like starting out with the assumption that it isn't going to work. There just wouldn't be enough commitment."

One man reported on his friend's prenuptial agreement: "After five years this guy tore it up. That was part of the agreement. But now he tells me, when they have an argument, the thought goes through his mind that maybe he should have hung on to it. I would never do that. I wouldn't want to feel I was holding a sword over someone's head."

Although the prenuptial agreement may seem like an easy solution to some, most men and women view it with ambivalence. On the one hand, there is a desire to protect one's economic interest, but on the other, there is a very traditional feeling that says you can't put a price tag on love.

3

Changing Expectations

*I*t seems that just about nothing is more private and individualized than deciding whom you will choose to date, when you will date, and if you are ready to be married. Right? Wrong! In fact, throughout history, the nature of intimate relationships, the establishment of formal unions, and even childbearing decisions have been dictated by the structure of society at the time.

Throughout our interviews, it was common for singles to compare their own situation with that of their parents, grandparents, and even earlier generations. We were told how much easier they had had it, with all of the benefits of rural life, including extended families, ice cream socials, and other traces of Americana that might have been depicted in a Norman Rockwell painting. While it is true that there have been some striking differences in patterns of mating and dating over the past two hundred years—even the past twenty —the underlying similarities remain.

Turning Back the Hands of Time

What was it like to be young and single in colonial America? To call them swinging singles would be an overstatement—but young people did have a surprising amount of control over their marital destiny. Even the Puritans, defined in Webster's New World Dictionary as "extremely or excessively strict in matters of morals and religion," recognized the human need for companionship and sexual satisfaction. What that translated into was: If little Polly Pureheart and Mr. John Smith were going to be married, they should have "a tendency to affection and sympathy" and time alone to discover if this was the case.

A woman's chances of being courted and getting married were linked to nothing more romantic than whether or not there was enough land available to support a new family unit. Eldest daughters were put at the top of the list for matrimony, and an enticing dowry usually clinched the deal. Parents and church held veto power over a person's marital choice, but in most cases parents controlled *when* not *whom* their children married.

Men did not marry until their mid- to late twenties; their brides were a few years younger. But young men and women began socializing together in their teenage years—and there were ample opportunities for this to occur. They were together in the one-room schoolhouse, in church, in the meetinghouse, and in the homes of their friends and relatives. The structures of church, school, and family discussed in chapter 1 were firmly in place.

Later on, as courtship progressed, they might even be together in bed—fully dressed, of course! Bundling, as this unique form of courtship was called, evolved in the mid-1700s as a way for couples to spend time with each other during the harsh winter months—when travel was difficult and fuel for heating was limited. The purpose was verbal, not sexual, intercourse. Although bundling operated on the honor system, not all parents were so trustful. A "bundling board" was sometimes placed in the middle of the bed to deter an amorous couple from prenuptial relations. However, the fact that about one-third of brides were pregnant during this time period casts considerable doubt on the effectiveness of such a barrier.

Marriage in the 1700s was a little like starting your own factory—right down to providing the raw materials. Consider what life was like at the time. The family unit (husband, wife, and children) had to produce and provide for all the needs of the family, including food, clothing, shelter, education, religious training, and recreation. Theoretically, women in the 1700s had few rights. They had no vote nor did they have the right to own property. Yet there was an egalitarian nature to the relationship between men and women because of the essential interdependency of their skills for survival. Men harvested the grain, women baked the bread; men sheared the sheep, women spun the wool.

So what constituted a good mate? For men, ownership of land was today's equivalent of an M.B.A. It was the sign of success and acceptability and a necessary precondition for courtship. For women, management and production skills were more important for their resume than a curvaceous figure and an endearing manner. Romantic love was a bonus—friendship and enduring companionship a must. In fact, pure romantic love was something to be wary of. It was thought to be unstable, self-indulgent, and a sign of immaturity. Life was filled with hard physical labor and many children. In the course of her married life, the New England wife bore an average of eight children and risked a one in thirty chance of dying as a result of each pregnancy. Although subordinate to the glory of God, sex within marriage was practically a holy sacrament. If Polly or John did not fulfill their conjugal obligation of sexual companionship, they could risk expulsion from the church. A good mate was one who successfully carried out his or her duties and responsibilities for the family. The fact of the matter is that regardless of personal differences or disappointments in the marital union, divorce was uncommon. Why? Alternative mate choices (especially for men) were scarce, the self-sufficiency of the home was dependent on the contributions of both people, and if that was not enough reason to stay together, there was a lot of geographical isolation—nowhere to run.

The Male-Female Split—There's No Place Like Home?

By the beginning of the nineteenth century, land supply in the East was dwindling. Farming and large families were on the way out. Many men packed their bags full of hope, skill, and courage to heed the call "go west young man," while others traded sickle and scythe for quill pen and ledger.

The reorganization of the work world not only affected *where* and *how* people earned a living, but altered the very nature of relationships between men and women. With economic production removed from the family unit, men and women were relegated to increasingly separate domains. The balance of power in relationships shifted drastically under this new arrangement. Now women were totally dependent on men for their livelihood and social position. The husband and wife duet of colonial America became solo performances: He made the money, she made the beds.

The new goal for women was primarily to make husbands happy. In exchange for a roof over her head, a woman was to provide her man with a clean retreat from the clamor and harshness of the work world. According to *Godey's Lady's Magazine*—the *Cosmopolitan* of the 1800s—the modern woman was expected to possess personal endowments that emphasized "purity of mind, simplicity and frankness of heart, benevolence, prompting to active charity, warm affection... forbearance and self denial...." Imagine the enormity of this role transition for women. Just as a whole new world was opening up for men, theirs was closing down.

By the mid-1800s, expectations for love had changed. How-to books, most of which were written for women, preached that young girls should marry for love, not money or status. Romantic love was now perceived as clearly superior to friendship and as a necessary condition for marriage. There was a tremendous desire to know more about what this love was, but young women wouldn't find it in a textbook. They found it between the covers—of a fat, juicy novel. The love story became the mainstay of popular culture.

In the mid-nineteenth century, romantic love was not synonomous with hearing bells or feeling uncontrollable passion, but was manifested by an appreciation for each other's thoughts and character. As one nineteenth-century woman wrote to her courter, "My heart is a castle with most obstinate doors...you have a right to enter in, explore, and know all the recesses of my heart."

In some respects, while courtship brought men and women together, marriage kept them apart. Prior to marriage, men and women generally joined in group activities—on walks, at parties, at church, or around the piano at someone's home. More serious courtship took place in the parlor, where young couples were left on their own. By this time, parents were out of the picture in terms of controlling the courtship of their children. This change is indicated in a letter from the times:

> Lizzie's sister did not go to bed until ten o'clock, after which my beloved and I went down, made a fire, and sat down to talk and kiss and embrace and bathe in love.

Men who found love and could afford marriage were eager to tie the knot; it was women who dragged their feet. It's no wonder they were apprehensive. While courtship brought closeness, sharing, communication, and intimacy, marriage brought separation, dependency, and risk. Women were separated from their families, and their well-being was tied to the business acumen of their husbands, who operated in a capitalist world from which women were excluded. Men were shopkeepers, clerks, cashiers, and managers. Women were watchdogs over morality, sexuality, and the psyche of their husbands—all within the confines of the home. According to Victorian standards, women had no sex drive: They had only a duty to engage in sex when necessary—primarily for procreative purposes. By 1860, the average fertility of white women was down to 5.21 children, although the abortion rate was on the rise.

Recognizing the unique sacrifices that women made when

choosing to marry, one man asked his fiancée, "Have you thought that you must leave all: home, friends, and every acquaintance and share you know not what, have you thought about the misery that the married woman may endure, her confinement to the house and her duties?" Put in those terms, it's hard to imagine that any woman in her right mind would agree to marry.

Making Progress

In the late 1800s and into the twentieth century, the key words were urbanization and industrialization. By the year 1880, one in four Americans lived in cities. The homogeneity of the rural settlement was replaced by an ever-expanding assortment of people. The person living next door could now be a stranger from another town or city; you no longer knew anything about his or her parents or background—nothing about habits or values. American life was forever transformed.

The formal worlds of men and women once again began to intersect. Coeducational public high schools and colleges began to spring up across the country. By 1900, females accounted for 40 percent of all college graduates. And what did they do with their education?

Women—especially immigrant women—entered the paid labor force in unprecedented numbers. Working-class families needed the extra money that a woman could earn in industries such as garment making, cigar rolling, and food processing. Whether it was through long days in factory sweatshops or even longer days doing piecework at home, the work of immigrant women kept their families from the brink of financial disaster. American employers were eager to hire the cheap labor that these women represented. The result was that their twenty-four-hour day was like a work marathon. A woman labored at an underpaid job, cleaned the house, cooked the meals, mothered her children, attended to her husband—and if she was really lucky, caught a few hours of sleep.

Many educated, middle-class, single women became teachers, nurses, or librarians. Others transported their maternal and nurturant qualities beyond the home and into the larger society. They became social workers and social reformers—helping the sick and poor, organizing unions and strikes, rebelling against unsanitary working conditions, and fighting for women's right to vote.

But the blurring of the boundary between men and women did not make meeting one another any easier. In fact, it became more difficult. Men and women were at school together, but they were not in the same classes. It was gender not brains or interest that determined what course of study men and women would follow. The employment situation further reflected the separate paths of the sexes: There were jobs for women and there were jobs for men. The camaraderie of the rural, one-room schoolhouse or the teamwork of the colonial couple was a far cry from the new scenario.

Life in the cities brought together single men and women from different classes and geographical areas. The business of finding a mate was becoming more complicated. Women who worked and lived alone in the city were more likely to be on their guard against men they didn't know. Their next-door neighbor might be an attractive, eligible bachelor, but who could be sure he wasn't Jack the Ripper? Women living in boardinghouses or female students living in dormitories were under strict surveillance. Informal contact was no longer very informal. Of women courting between 1870 and 1910, 11 percent never married, the highest proportion in American history. Many of these women were unwilling to give up their profession for the constraints of married life. Others were willing but were deemed unacceptable as marriage partners because they were too educated. A college-educated woman was more than some men could handle.

The separateness of men and women permitted their fantasies and imaginations to run wild. Romantic love was once again redefined. This time it appeared in all of its irrational, idealized glory. The knight in shining armor had come out of the pages of romantic novels and into the hearts and dreams of American women. The new ideal man was not to be your ordinary knight but rather a delicate balance of chivalry, gentleness, and aggression. Women of these times were waiting for love—and love was believed to strike with an unmistakable force that would leave no doubt as to its existence. Unfortunately, there was a lot of doubt as women tried to reconcile their expectations for love with their actual experiences.

Despite all the activity of women outside the home, domesticity was still the norm. But the family was continually shrinking in size and new technologies were making women's work less physically demanding.

Love on Wheels

Take a young man and woman and a Model T and what do you get? "Pregnant," might have been the wry response of many early-twentieth-century parents. That is not too far from the truth. But while parked cars with fogged-up windows were not an uncommon sight, the limit was generally set at heavy petting, not intercourse. The automobile was like a bedroom on wheels: It allowed couples unprecedented freedom and privacy—far away from the watchful eyes of parents, neighbors, and friends. According to the Kinsey Report, the greatest increase in premarital sexual activity occurred within the first two decades of the twentieth century—but it was expected to be reserved for those who were engaged. Men, of course, were guided by the double standard that allowed them greater latitude in their premarital sexual activities.

Dating, as an activity separate from courtship, evolved in

the 1920s. Unlike the courtship of earlier years, dating was an institution in and of itself, with no necessary ties to matrimony. It was described as a "dalliance"—a time of fun and experimentation. A great date was good-looking, popular, and had "wheels." But a good catch was more than just a fun time or a show-stopping dance partner; he or she was a ticket to increased prestige. The big man on campus needed just the right woman in the passenger seat of his Oldsmobile.

Where did they go on a Friday night? Trains, streetcars, and automobiles opened up a whole new world of entertainment possibilities. Social events that were miles away were now fair game for dating couples. Young people socialized in dance halls, cabarets, and movie theaters. But the cheek-to-cheek dances and dark movie houses were more conducive to increased sexuality than to sharing the inner recesses of one's mind.

The key word of the 1920s was *consumerism*. The female stereotype of piety and purity went out as the new image of the flapper danced its way in. With the advances in contraceptive technology came relaxed sexual mores. Popular magazines now preached that sexual repression was psychologically unhealthy for both sexes. The booming advertising industry flooded the market with images of the new American woman: smoking cigarettes, dancing flirtatiously, and kissing unabashedly. This new woman kicked away the pedestal that she had been put upon, rid herself of those who would worship her, and set out to live life to its fullest.

One of the repercussions of the age of consumerism and advertising was the commercial "packaging" of women. The thin, flat-chested image of the flapper was the rage—and many women resorted to dieting, exercising, and even binding their breasts. The cosmetic industry burst on the scene with soaps, deodorants, mouthwashes, and shampoos that no woman could afford to be without. Ponds Cream, Palmolive Soap, and Woodbury Shampoo promised greater popularity, charm, and romance.

More and more women left rural areas for life alone in the cities. Some found work as salesladies or clerical workers; others continued their education. By 1920, approximately 30 percent of all college presidents and professors, 5 percent of all physicians, and 1 percent of the lawyers and judges were women.

One thing was for certain: Women were not having lots of babies. The birthrate of the 1920s plummeted. It was a time of political and social freedom for women. Marriage remained an important goal, but women were looking for greater equality in that realm, too. The divorce rate was over 50 percent higher in 1920 than it had been in 1910.

Love in War and Peace

Something was added to the uniform of thousands of young men who served in World War II—a wedding band. With war's threat of separation and death, dating became a serious business—with matrimony as the goal. On the home front, women were needed in every profession, in every factory. The marriage rate and the birthrate soared. Between 1940 and 1950, nineteen million babies were born.

The tenuousness and sobriety of wartime America left its mark on social relations for a decade to follow. Security, home, and family became the hallmark of the 1950s. Women who had entered traditionally male occupations during the war were abruptly fired when the war ended. Women had returned to the home and hearth and maternity ward. The virtuous woman with a flair for domesticity was once more crowned the ideal female.

Women who did not follow this dictate faced a difficult and unsupportive environment. A classic 1950s film, *The Red Shoes*, provides an extreme example: The heroine, torn between the awesome choice of love or her career as a ballerina, is driven to suicide.

The popular image of women that now popped out of the

magazine pages and off the movie screen enticed women to alter their body in new ways. A full, round bosom reflected the maternal woman of the 1950s. If you weren't naturally endowed with the full-figured look, you could purchase a padded bra or start bust development exercises. The advertising industry jumped on the bandwagon of motherhood and domesticity by using pictures of mothers and babies in the majority of their advertising copy. Mothers were displayed in starched dresses and aprons—touting the whiteness of their wash and the shine of their pots and pans.

Being in love and going steady were important goals for young men and women of the 1950s, and the high school and college campuses were the most likely meeting places. But despite their increased education and training, women of the 1950s were taught to play dumb. This new image of womanhood was propagated by books such as *The Power of Sexual Surrender*. Women's magazines featured articles such as "Manners and Morals," "Support Your Husband's Career," "Motherhood Is a Way of Life," and "She Doesn't Keep House the Way I Do." Even little children got the message. No self-respecting mother would have been without Dr. Spock's treatise on baby care and child rearing, in which he urged mothers and fathers to display stereotypical behaviors of masculinity and femininity so that their children would grow up to fulfill their appropriate roles in life. Ozzie and Harriet Nelson and June and Ward Cleaver were sterling models of this all-American family.

Revolution

The passive woman of the 1950s was not very palatable to her sister of the late 1960s. In fact, young people were disillusioned with much of what they saw around them: racial inequality, poverty, and a senseless, unpopular war. Hard on the heels of the civil rights movement came the antiwar movement. Through organization and demonstrations, the will of the youthful, active, socially aware, was pitted against that of the established order. By the time the Vietnam war ended, a new target had emerged: gender equality —not sexual equality, because the goal was broader than that—to open operating rooms, legal practices, and corporate boardrooms to women, with the same rights and income as the males who occupied them.

In 1966, the National Organization of Women (NOW) was founded, primarily by career women, to systematically fight labor inequalities. Research had demonstrated the reality, shocking to many, that occupational segregation by gender was no different in 1960 than it had been in 1900.

The women's liberation movement, which was begun on college campuses by younger, middle-class students, broadened NOW's focus to include a host of other women's issues such as legalized abortion, day-care, and sexual equality. Women were seeking self-satisfaction and the removal of the double standard that had existed for centuries in the sexual behavior of men and women—and the pill was an important tool. It gave women the freedom to fulfill their own sexual needs without fear of pregnancy. Now love, not a diamond ring, legitimized premarital intercourse for both sexes.

The media had a field day with the changing mores and new life-styles. Magazines specifically devoted to the career woman—such as *Working Woman* and *Savvy*—entered the market. Articles featuring clean homes and healthy babies were replaced by "The Pill and the Girl Next Door," "About the Divorcée," and "The Dating Bar."

Simone de Beauvoir's *The Second Sex* and Betty Friedan's *The Feminine Mystique* became the bibles of those moving toward feminism. Friedan criticized the domesticity of women, arguing that in the long run, children benefited more from a mother who had a sense of self and a life of her own. Helen Gurley Brown took a different tack in *Sex and the Single Girl* by urging women to use their sexuality for their own advancement. She preached that "sex is a power-

47

ful weapon for a single woman in getting what she wants from life, a husband or steady male companionship." According to Brown, "A single woman who doesn't deny her body regularly and often to get what she wants is an idiot." In other words, a woman should withhold sex to have power over men.

In the 1960s a number of forces came into play that altered the mate selection process. The credo of the times was anti compromise, anti commitment, and pro me—not exactly the sentiments that mesh two people in a long-term relationship. Women were trying out new roles and so were men. As the subordinate sex, women were demanding more; but as the superordinate sex, men were trying to free themselves of the John Wayne, Superman, and breadwinner images. They were seeking to unlock the door to that area of humanity that defied the traditional credo of manhood and defined the realm of womanhood. Across the country, men (albeit a minority) were getting together in consciousness-raising groups to support one another in the struggle to change seemingly inborn behaviors and self-expectations. By 1971, even Dr. Spock was recanting the sexist advice in his books on child care!

Women's Lib—Look at Me Now

The women's movement had a difficult birth and adolescence. It grew and stretched and tested its boundaries, while new rhetoric and codes of behavior continually evolved. Most discussions of women's lib focus on the long-term effects that we see around us now as the movement has entered maturity, such as greater opportunity and equality in the work world and new standards for behavior on the home front. But what about the effect on the millions of women who were caught in the whirlwind of changing norms and expectations—trying to incorporate new values and goals into their immediate life decisions?

For middle-class, educated women who already had liberal

leanings, there was pressure to make their mark on the world. By adding to that a circle of female friends who were of a similar mindset, you gained the support and camaraderie to forge ahead and do what was "right" for a woman of a new era.

Denise, a thirty-six-year-old computer salesperson, told us she feels angry and victimized by her current single status. As an undergraduate and graduate student throughout most of her twenties, she was strongly influenced by the teachings of the women's movement. A woman had to grab from the world what she could while she could still do it—free from the constraints of a long-term commitment to a man.

Denise had few periods in her life when she was not involved with a man—a man that she really cared about. But with a deep breath and a lot of apprehension she left these relationships in order to pursue her education and career. Looking back now, Denise feels both pride and anger—pride in her many accomplishments and anger at a very heartfelt void in her life. At thirty-six, she wants a husband and children.

Throughout our interviews, we heard the frustrated voices of single women in their early to late thirties who felt they were paying a steep price for their position in history. Leah, a thirty-two-year-old audiologist, told us, "I look at myself and I think, 'Hey, I'm a pretty neat person—what's going on here?' I'm director of my department at the hospital, I'm respected by my colleagues and all of my friends. So when do I get the other perks [husband, kids, etc.]?"

On Mother's Day last year, Jill, a thirty-five-year-old pediatrician, was waiting to cross the street in downtown Denver. A young girl who looked about eleven or twelve years old wished her a happy Mother's Day and then—as an instinctive check on the validity of her statement—asked her if she was a mother. Jill looked at the girl, hesitated for a second, and then smiled and replied, "No, I'm not." To hear Jill tell us about it you would think she had been interrogated by the CIA. "I know it's crazy that that incident is so clear in my mind," she told us, "but the little girl's question hit me in my most vulnerable spot. I sacrificed so much to get where I am today and I have a lot to be proud of. But one question like that and I feel like I'm defective—like I'm inadequate."

Women expressed the feeling of having been deceived, of having been duped into believing that they would be rewarded with more than an impressive résumé and the ability to succeed in the world of work. Women who had broken through the gender barrier and competed with men for the good positions were not always happy with their discoveries. Professional women found old-boy networks, relentless scrutiny of their performance, and a set of business ethics that they were not prepared for or necessarily willing to incorporate. Women never wanted to take on the characteristics of men in order to succeed. They hoped instead to infiltrate the institutions of society with their own brand of competence, achievement, and style.

Some women feel the women's movement strengthened them to make decisions about relationships and career that they would have been unable or unwilling to make before. Others resent the pressure they felt to deny "needing" a man and making personal decisions primarily as loyal followers of a movement. The common denominator for women is the feeling that things could have been done differently—that loving, compromising, and self-advancement were not mutually exclusive goals.

Tall, Dark, and Handsome

"The older I get the more I sound like a lawyer reading a bill of rights. I want to know up front where a relationship is going, what's in it for me, how important it will be in the scheme of things." Welcome to the 1980s.

Two words have become associated with mating and dating in the 1980s—*anxiety* and *rationality*—and they are not unrelated. The high divorce rates of the previous decade and the onslaught of sexually transmitted diseases have made getting together "till death do us part" something to think about in more ways than one. Relationships have become risky business and high anxiety the price. This is personified in the hit movie *Fatal Attraction*, which graphically portrays the danger of letting your libido lead the way.

We are told by the popular press that rationality is the new approach. No more white knights, unrealistic expectations, or desires to change anyone's character. As one thirty-four-year-old woman told us, "I spent five years in therapy trying to convince myself that there was not a Mr. Perfect out there somewhere." Now people are looking for someone that they can be with for the long haul—they are looking for trust, stability, dependability, and commitment, and are willing to forgo the racing heartbeat. These sound like sentiments that would be shared by our colonial ancestors!

What are the changed expectations for a mate? Clearly there has been no role reversal between men and women. House husbands do exist, but they are definitely not the norm. Yes, men may do more of the vacuuming and change a few more diapers, but the bulk of the responsibility for housework and child care has always been and still is with the woman—regardless of whether she is home all day or works full-time in a professional position. Studies show that in most two-career marriages, even those without children, the husband's job will take priority when it comes to issues such as promotion and geographic relocation.

But some things have changed. Delayed marriage has meant more time to find and define ourselves as individuals. Technological advances have increased the amount of leisure time available to us. A general concern with psychological factors has added another category to our compatibility index. The cumulative effect of these factors has been to shake up our thinking about what we want, deserve, and should strive for in a mate—and the dust has still not settled. There is confusion about male and female roles and how two-career couples can creatively manage work, home, and family without one person feeling victimized. The increasing ability of both men and women to single-handedly provide for themselves has placed demands for a mate beyond the needs of day-to-day subsistence. Now we are looking for someone who can contribute to other dimensions of our lives: our thoughts, feelings, communicative abilities, intellect, hobbies, level of physical fitness. The list goes on and on and so does the search.

The new rational approach has not meant simply going back to the basics of finding a kind, dependable, trustworthy companion who makes a decent living—as if that weren't hard enough. But now two individuals and two established life-styles must mesh. That means that on first dates people are being sized up on very specific characteristics—like career, owner or renter status, what part of town they live in, what they do for fun, what kind of shape they're in, and—if it ever gets to date number two or three—their taste in furnishings, books, and style of cooking. The point is that people are trying their hardest to learn from the casualties of divorce, trying to cover all the bases, from character and values to income potential to day-to-day habits.

Jan, a beautiful thirty-three-year-old health care consultant, has been involved with a number of men but has never found anyone that she felt was Mr. Right. Much of her spare time is spent working out in gyms and training for the high level of competitive volleyball at which she competes. Since physical fitness is so important to her and volleyball, in particular, occupies so much of her time, she limits her selection of eligible mates to fellow volleyball jocks. But so far no one has been able to offer enough of the other qualities she wants in a mate: liberal political leanings, interest in activist groups such as Amnesty International, love of dogs, and someone who is emotionally stable, strong, sensitive, and vulnerable.

Clair grew up in a small town in the Pacific Northwest. Now twenty-eight, she recalls the traditional sex role expectations of her childhood: "Mom made it clear that I would go to college, then work for a few years so I would know what it was like for my husband, and be married by the time I was thirty. If you didn't make it by then, your chances were zilch. I grew up thinking I would marry, but now...I'm ambiguous. The older I get the less I want to give up. I find myself being a lot more judgmental about people—very selective—much quicker to say 'that person's not for me.'"

We are currently in the midst of a more conservative movement that is seeking to strike a balance between the restrictive norms of the 1950s and the seeming normlessness of the late 1960s and 1970s. However, we question whether the balance has been struck. One night after a two-hour focus group session with thirty-five to thirty-nine-year-old men and women, all we could do was sit and stare at one another in disbelief. *Rational* is too flippant a word to describe what we heard. Over and over throughout the evening the message was clear: "I don't want to be with somebody that I have to take care of," "I've worked hard for what I've got and I don't want to lose it." Especially for people who are well-established in their career, who own property or other valuable goods, there is concern about who is bringing what to the relationship. More women are earning six-figure salaries and demanding at least matching funds from a prospective mate.

Our brief overview of men's and women's roles over the last three centuries cannot be removed from the economic, political, legal, and normative context of the times of which they are a part. It may appear that men's roles have not really undergone any fundamental changes other than where men worked or what they worked at; that it is really women's roles that have had the roller coaster ride. To some extent, this is true. However, we could borrow the notion from physics that for every action there is a reaction, and apply it to the change in roles over time. The result is that the lives of men and women are so interconnected that a substantial change in the role of one sex will ultimately affect the other.

4

The New Intimacy

What *is* intimacy? Men and women differed sharply in their responses. The moment we introduced the topic of intimacy, males began talking about sexual activities, while females talked about feelings and emotions. That difference, in itself, revealed some of the age-old controversy and frequent misunderstanding between the sexes.

Before focusing on the "new" intimacy, the dramatic changes that have taken place for both sexes in the area of intimacy and intimate relationships, let's take a hard look at what we have left behind. What exactly was the "old" intimacy?

For us, the old intimacy refers to behavior and beliefs commonly held prior to the sexual revolution of the mid-1960s. The decade immediately preceding this preached sexual conservativism; according to the belief of the day, sexual intimacy was to be reserved for marriage only. In those days, "Does she or doesn't she?" didn't refer to changing one's hair color, and the social consensus was that she had better not.

The watchword of the dating scene in the fifties was *predictability*. Amy Vanderbilt's popular manual on dating etiquette, published in 1956, articulated the accepted practices of the day. Men were carefully lectured on their behavior; they were not only reminded to open and close doors, but they were told they must assume full financial responsibility for the evening's expenses—even in cases where the woman had extended the invitation. It was all a part of the dating rules, and everyone knew them.

Yet even then a certain double standard existed; males who broke dating rules were simply called forgetful or socially awkward, while women who did not abide by the rules were judged to be brash, desperate, and not very nice. But we must remember that part of that double standard was the shared recognition that women had much more to lose by a misstep.

A forty-eight-year-old surgery nurse told us, "If you were single and pregnant in the fifties, you had one of two choices: Marry the guy or move. Actually there was a third: You could wear the scarlet *A* and slink around town by yourself for the rest of your life."

For women, the bottom-line loss was premarital pregnancy, but the more subtle one, nearly as devastating for future prospects, was reputation. The delicate negotiations through the dating and prenuptial terrain revolved around female responsibility for keeping male passions under control. It may not sound like an ideal package, but at least everyone knew the contents.

Then Came the Revolution

When we asked men and women to describe their understanding of the term "sexual revolution," it was soon apparent it meant different things to different people. Comments ranged from skepticism and confusion to disillusionment.

Ben, a thirty-one-year-old commercial artist, told us, "Sure, I can describe the sexual revolution. It's a set of new rules that aren't so new anymore; values of justice, loyalty, and good sportsmanship have flown out the window."

Anna, a forty-two-year-old travel editor, remarked with a touch of wistfulness, "It was a good idea that went wrong."

Jeff, a thirty-six-year-old financial planner, commented, "The sexual revolution—sometimes I ask myself, did it really happen, or did we just read about it in the paper?"

Often the most sophisticated men and women voiced a

surprising regret at changes they had vocally supported in the past. Jill, a thirty-two-year-old attorney, remarked, "I never expected it to be like this, damn it—it's not very lady-like. I have the feeling we really sold out, that we thought we were serving our own best interests; but we lost on a lot of fronts, without getting anything in return. It's like making a bad real estate deal—it looks great on paper, until you start reading the fine print."

Who is giving us the most accurate picture? Is there a right view and a wrong view? Was there a revolution or not?

In Webster's New World Dictionary, the definition of "revolution" as the sudden overthrow of a government or social system is *eighth* in a long list of meanings. The first refers to the orbital movement of heavenly bodies, including the sun and stars.

Although the term "sexual revolution" is generally understood in the context of an overthrow of existing values, closer examination reveals the so-called revolution to have been the product of a more gradual development. The seeds that bore the fruit of change were sown nearly half a century before.

In the early 1900s we saw the post-Victorian shedding of sexual restrictions, which had sometimes deteriorated into sheer silliness. For example, at the height of the modesty mania, even table legs were hidden by skirts, lest they remind one of the corresponding female appendages.

Nevertheless, it was not until the roaring twenties, which for some was the "decade of decadence," that sexual intimacy *within* marriage was fully approved. The new expectation even found its way into some marriage manuals, which began to discuss sex as a means of *mutual* fulfillment. This heralded the beginning of the radical idea that sexual behavior could be a valuable part of intimate relationships per se. From our perspective, this may seem inconsequential. But if you cast a quick eye at the long history of denigrating sex via concubine, mistress, harlot, and prostitute, and the tradition prohibiting women from seeking sexual satisfaction from their husbands, the change was monumental.

Some argue that the sexual revolution was primarily a convergence of sexual behavior with changing attitudes. But history shows the two seldom converge. If we trace attitudes vs. behavior, we see that behavior generally lags behind: By the time behavior catches up, attitudes have shifted, usually in order to "adjust" to the changed behavior. The process is never static.

While Victorian morality still had people concerned with hiding ankles, church records, coupled with data from elderly women in the 1948 Kinsey studies, indicate that about one-fourth of brides up to the early 1900s were nonvirgins. From the 1920s through the 1950s, a period of increased recognition of the valid place of sexuality in *marriage*, the proportion of women experiencing *premarital* intercourse rose from 25 to 50 percent.

The 1960s heralded the most drastic attitude change toward sexual behavior in U.S. history. This was the decade of political activism, the women's movement, and the pill. While parental influence decreased due to changing family structures, peer influence increased, and the figure for premarital intercourse for women jumped to nearly 75 percent. The sexual revolution had arrived.

On paper the concept is a simple one: freedom for men and women alike, to enact the sexual behaviors of their choice, without society's interference in the form of social snickering and finger pointing. For some, the new freedom meant they could engage more easily in serious, intimate relationships without marriage. For others, the primary message of the sexual revolution was that voiced by a thirty-four-year-old male accountant, "If it feels good, do it—score, score, score!"

The changes we have come to regard as part of a sexual revolution might more accurately be viewed as a social revolution. Maggie, a thirty-seven-year-old pediatrician, noted,

"Women were demanding sexual equality as a political statement; sex really wasn't the major issue at all. It was more to
show that we could make the same free choices about our
sexual behavior. If men could be aggressive, so could we. I
must admit it didn't turn out quite the way a lot of women
had expected."

The increasing rate of premarital intercourse for women
was only a rough indicator of the immensity of the change
that began in the sixties. Relying on percentage alone, one
could argue that, since the rates (for premarital intercourse)
had already doubled from the early 1900s to the 1950s, another 25 percent increase wasn't a big deal. The "big deal"
is, first, that the latter change took place over a relatively
brief time period and, second, that for the first time in our
history a clear majority of women were engaging in sexual
behavior prior to marriage. In addition, the rates only capture the "did she or didn't she" behavior. Given what we
already know about the fifties and before, it is most likely
that women who engaged in premarital sex did so on a one-
partner basis, and usually ended up marrying that partner.
The general attitude toward sexual intimacy remained that it
was taboo outside marriage, with the possible exception of
the almost married (engaged or "going steady").

The most sobering aspect of changes in sexual behavior in
the sixties is not the behavior itself, but the attitude change it
represents. For the first time in our history, sexual behavior
outside marriage has not only come to be *accepted*, but frequently *expected* as well. The pressure of this expectation
opens what used to be assumed, at least in the beginning of a
relationship, to be a closed issue. Women can no longer
claim the protection of an unspoken morality as sufficient
reason for sexual abstinence. As a result, women are angry
that men do not understand that intimacy is "not just sex,"
and men resent women "wanting to make such a big thing
out of it."

Sarah, a thirty-five-year-old court reporter, told us, "I

don't know why men find it so hard to understand. You need to establish intimacy in order to enjoy sex. I can't just go out with a man and go to bed with him. That would only come after knowing someone for a long time, and trusting him."

Carole, a thirty-one-year-old swimming coach, remarked, "You talk about winning and losing—I'm definitely losing. I look at the men I'm putting out for, and I think 'What the hell is wrong with me?' I feel like I've been in a string of one-night stands. But that's what guys are pushing for."

On the other hand, although the sexual revolution may appear to be a Garden of Eden for men, the reality is that for the first time they find themselves on the receiving end of pressure to engage in sex. Scott, a thirty-one-year-old physicist, remarked, "Now I know what women used to complain about. It really feels crummy when you think someone just wants to have sex—it's like you could be anyone—it wouldn't matter, just so your body has the right parts."

Cid, a forty-three-year-old systems analyst, told us, "It sounds funny, because guys are supposed to be such easy turn-ons, but it's a weird feeling when women are the aggressors—that's real pressure. What if you can't produce? It makes you start to wonder a little about your masculinity. I'm not saying it happens that way all the time—but it only takes once."

The fact that single men and women know they are free to engage in sexual behavior without social reprisals seems to have driven a mental wedge between them. Although their differences often appear to revolve around the issue of sex, we were told over and over that "sex is only the tip of the iceberg."

And indeed, when all the stops were out, something unforeseen happened. Removing sexual tension as a major source of conflict between men and women did not leave the sexes in blissful harmony. Instead, it seemed to heighten animosity. The focus of the problem moved to less concrete ground, and confusion intensified. If you had a fight, it was because he was a "sexist pig," or she was a "rabid feminist," whatever those were. All the petty arguments and daily annoyances that arise in any close relationship now assumed a political dimension. To be remiss in a phone call, to forget his birthday, to dislike her favorite music, was no longer one-on-one bickering; it was a part of the global war of the sexes. You could scarcely have an old-fashioned argument about socks in the sink or mistreatment of your favorite record album, without it becoming part of a rhetoric of sexual exploitation (his or hers) or a failure to contribute to your growth as an individual. It seemed the new freedom in sexual behaviors had, instead of commingling harmony and love, simply heated up the battle of the sexes.

In this case, singles appear to have fallen victim to the old Irish curse, "May you get everything that you ask for." Probably nothing is more disillusioning than getting your heart's desire and finding that it not only doesn't make your problems go away, it may aggravate them as well.

Both men and women had high hopes that the loosening of sexual restrictions would remove the major stumbling block between them. What they failed to realize is that sexual activity cannot be divorced from the complex of history, tradition, economics, and the individual psyche.

Pink Lady in a Red Dress

Historically woman has been classified as one of two extremes: saint or sinner. As saint, woman was present in the goddess worship of ancient civilization, in images of fertility, regeneration, and beauty. From Astarte to Aphrodite to Mary, mother of Jesus, we have been presented with a model of perfection in womanhood.

But predating the goddess image is another: the dark spectral form of woman as temptress. Eve, the fallen consort, is held responsible for the exile of the entire human race from paradise; and almost as old as the story of Eve is that of Pandora, the first mortal woman, sent by Zeus to punish mankind for the theft of fire by Prometheus. Just as Eve could not resist the apple, Pandora could not resist lifting the lid of the box left in her charge, releasing all of the world's misfortunes to plague us forever. Once again, paradise was lost—by the feminine touch.

It is little wonder that, even from antiquity, women have been blamed for the moral failings of men. Men were off the hook because they could not be expected to withstand those powerful, mysterious forces exerted upon them by the magic of womankind.

And what has this image meant for women? Basically, that their misfortunes have been viewed, in some mysterious way, as their own fault. Lucretia, child-wife of a Roman nobleman, whose ultimate fate is depicted so movingly in the Rembrandt painting that bears her name, is a classic example. Raped by Sextus, the king's son, she was honor bound to do "the manly thing," which was to kill herself to save her husband from disgrace. In the painting we see the knife blade plunged into her heart by her own hand, destroying the "spoiled possession" that would have been a continuing embarrassment to all.

Regardless of which image was attributed to a woman, she was in a no-win situation. One answer to the problem was for women to appear as similar to men as possible, to finally rid themselves of the ancient stereotypes. But women quickly discovered that playing by the same sexual rules as men did nothing to change the deep-seated differences in sexuality between male and female.

The Pill—Liberation in a Packet

For women, the birth control pill was the antibiotic of pregnancy. For the first time a woman could behave with exactly the same carefree attitude in the bedroom as a man;

there was no need to excuse herself from a passionate embrace to head for the bathroom for preparations at a tender moment, or to be burdened with worry over an accidental pregnancy. The pill was the key to freedom for women; it meant the ability to control their own biology, to have a viable alternative to the male dictum—not always rendered with humor—"keep 'em barefoot in winter and pregnant in summer."

Even preliterate societies were concerned with birth control; but for them, abortion and infanticide proved more effective in limiting population. This is hardly surprising, given the state of their knowledge and the techniques at their disposal. For example, one birth control method involved taking a length of twisted bark and dipping it in egg yolk; but since it was subsequently hung around the neck, it was not very effective.

Although the later Greek and Roman civilizations displayed some knowledge of conception and knew that prolonged lactation reduced fertility, it was not until the early nineteenth century that more reliable methods emerged. During this period the process of vulcanizing rubber became sufficiently developed to produce condoms and diaphragms. Modern birth control was on its way.

The development of birth control devices in the 1900s divided organizations and individuals into two opposing camps: for and against. Arguments ranged from issues of morality to economic issues involving the pros and cons of population control.

Despite objections in various sectors, public opinion favoring birth control continued to grow. In a 1938 *Ladies' Home Journal* poll, 79 percent of respondents favored the use of birth control. A factor fueling opinion in the 1930s was, of course, the Great Depression.

In the 1950s, the threat of overpopulation loomed as the next major social crisis, and attitudes toward birth control became increasingly favorable. It was in this climate that the pill was developed. In 1955 the first human testing of the pill proved successful. In 1960 the U.S. Food and Drug Administration authorized its use amid a certain amount of controversy; this was the first time medication would be prescribed, on a routine basis, for reasons that did not relate to maintaining good health and/or staving off disease. Some viewed it with the same alarm as operating on a healthy body.

Interestingly enough, early feminists were opposed to birth control, fearing it would lead to the sexual exploitation of women by men. Later feminists praised it as marking the biological liberation of women. Women today are not so sure. One of the most frequent opinions we heard was that voiced by a thirty-four-year-old speech therapist, who told us, "I think we [women] made *one big* mistake! Once you go to bed with a guy that's it. The talking is over. All he wants to do after that is head for the bedroom. We bought all that crap about sexual freedom. What it really means is now men expect to get you in bed without putting themselves out in the least: no more of the little courtesies—like five minutes of conversation."

Strangers in the Bedroom

There is no doubt that removing the difficulty of obtaining sex has had an enormous impact on men and women alike, but it has done little to improve the sense of understanding between them. Sexuality, as an expression of mutual intimacy, involves a sharing of the emotional, psychological, and physical selves. The two components of intimacy are sexual intimacy, which is a property of the individual, and emotional intimacy, which is a property of the relationship. In the past, women have been the acknowledged gatekeepers of sexual activity within a relationship. This was based, in part, on the fact that sexual activity was a riskier enterprise for them. Today one might argue that since neither their reputation nor risk of pregnancy is any great consideration, women have relinquished this role. Or perhaps there is no longer a need for gatekeepers, because there are no longer any gates.

In his best-selling book, *The Closing of the American Mind*, Allan Bloom laments the indifference of American students, expressed in what he calls a "flatness" of preferences and character. This extends to their relationships, often characterized by what one student summed up for him as the current ivy league assessment of sexual behavior: "It's no big deal."

Bloom's commentary, threaded throughout his book, suggests that life, including sexuality, is what you make it, and American students increasingly lack the tools to make it into very much at all. Their "passion" has withered before ever coming into flower. Whether the tools should be provided by school, family, or a broader culture may be a matter of debate, but few would dispute they are missing.

We were especially interested in Bloom's report of the student comment about sex, since in the interviews we conducted we heard the same assessment of sexual activity, in almost exactly the same words: "It's no big deal." We would argue that it is a "big deal," and that part of the difficulty men and women are experiencing in intimate relationships today comes from having bought into the belief that it is not. The attempt to obliterate the very real differences in the experience of the sexual act for men and women has led people to underestimate the awesome power of sex and human sexuality in shaping their lives. One of the most unfortunate by-products of the sexual revolution has been its success in trivializing sex.

Although the impact of Freud's work on the future of psychology is still under debate, today's adults remain products of a general conviction that repressed sexuality is responsible for a variety of social ills. The inferential leap for many has been that a society without sexual self-consciousness will be truly free. But when the inference was translated into action, men and women found themselves in midair, without a net to break their fall.

According to singles we interviewed, sexual freedom has been marked more by confusion than liberation. Why? What exactly is the problem? How do we identify and articulate it? And most important, who are the respondents? In issues of sexual behavior and emotional intimacy, it is not enough to identify respondents as single men and women: It matters enormously whether they have ever been married, for how long, and for how long they have been single. A thirty-seven-year-old mother of two, fresh out of a twelve-year-old marriage, is going to answer questions on intimacy far differently than a twenty-eight-year-old, never-married, male attorney. Each new wave of first-time mate seekers will have a different set of expectations than those looking the second time around. Age, sex, and past experience all exert a significant influence. Whether singles are over eighteen but under twenty-five, over thirty but not yet forty, or over fifty, they bring a unique past, cultural outlook, and history of relationships to bear on present expectations.

But regardless of age or background, the sense of uncertainty and the need to protect oneself from hurt or exploitation, was commonly expressed. A thirty-eight-year-old building contractor told us, "I still haven't figured out why my wife walked out on me. I've gone to a few seminars and workshops on male consciousness raising. They were helpful. When I listen to what other guys are saying, I feel less guilty, less as though it must have been something I did. I'm beginning to think more and more that women are really screwed up. They say they want one thing, you give it to them, and they want something else. How do you ever know where you stand?"

Sheila, a thirty-four-year-old commercial artist, commented, "Men always think of sex as the great problem solver. They are the real romantics—in a very unrealistic way. One of my favorite Woody Allen scenes is where he goes off with Mia Farrow for the 'great experience' they never had twelve years before. It's in the woods—the perfect romantic setting. The next day it shows her with a terrible headache from all the frogs croaking, and Woody is saying, 'Was it as bad as I thought?' That's more like the way it really is most of the time."

Ken, a thirty-two-year-old, never-married pharmacist, described one solution to frustrating relationships. "Celibacy—I really mean it. I know it used to be a word reserved for monks and old men, but there's something to it. I went through a period where I had dated so many women, and was feeling so crummy, that I decided to take a good, long time-out. I think I was relying too much on having women tell me who I was. I needed to be by myself for a while. I still went out with people, but just as friends, and did a lot of group things—softball, volleyball, parties where I went alone and left by myself. That lasted for about a year. Now I feel different about myself—better—but the women I'm seeing seem to be at the same place they were before."

Cara, a twenty-eight-year-old travel agent, told us, "I've dated a lot, but I've never been very satisfied. I really don't know what men want. A few months ago I went to a sexuality workshop for women. It made me think a lot more about what sex means. In male terms, sex is something you do *to* someone else. In female terms it's something you do *with* someone else. A woman's sexuality is different in another way too: It's something that is with her all the time, an approach to life. They told us the original meaning of the word *virgin* in Greek was 'unto yourself.' An unmarried woman was someone who took that energy and used it for herself. I think men sense something about the power we have, and it scares them. Our sexuality isn't only physical, it's spiritual, too."

Marilyn, a thirty-three-year-old public relations director, told us, "We think we've come a long way, but in many ways we're deluding ourselves. My friends still wait around for guys to call—even when the guys make a big deal out of getting their number in the first place. I won't do that. The last relationship I was in I negotiated like a contract: We would be together until a certain date and if things weren't working out, we could cancel the contract, but not before then. I can't stand the hassle of who will be in and out of my life. It takes too much energy."

Bart, a twenty-nine-year-old legal assistant, told us, "A lot depends on the place sex has in a relationship. Sometimes I get the feeling women don't know how to enjoy sex. They just know how to use it—as a reward, or to prove commitment. They never just do it."

As we noted at the beginning of this chapter, when we began to explore the topic of sexuality and intimacy in our interviews, we discovered that definitions differed enormously for men and women. If we used the word *intimacy* by itself, males assumed immediately that we were talking about sexual intimacy, and began to respond as though that was the question. Women responded to the question as one of emotional closeness. As a result, we divided the question into two parts: We asked about issues of emotional intimacy on the one hand, and issues of sexual behavior on the other. For us, this phenomenon dramatized the fact that men *do* view sexual behavior as intimacy, while women separate the two and generally seek to establish emotional intimacy prior to sexual behavior. This can be a painful source of confusion for both males and females seeking a relationship.

For men, issues of intimacy are primarily a matter of "let me show you how I feel," while for women they are "let's talk about it." The saying, "You can't live with 'em and you can't live without 'em," neatly summarizes the conflict between need and exasperation that was constantly expressed, by both men and women, in the course of our interviews.

The need for intimacy is a vital one for human beings, but the pursuit of it seems to be a risky business. By analogy, one of the most dangerous places in the jungle is the watering hole, where every animal, large or small, strong or weak, must come to drink. Yet at the very moment an animal lowers its head to the water, it is most vulnerable to attack. The need for intimacy is a little like that: You will never be as exposed, never as open to wounding, as when you are seeking to fill this need. Ironically, the degree of intimacy you achieve is directly connected to the degree to which you permit this exposure, with all its dangers.

Delilah with Muscles

There was a time, not so very long ago, when the differences between the sexes were set down in very definite terms. We knew unequivocally that little girls were soft and gentle, that boys were rough and tough, and that both must be treated accordingly. As the well-known nursery rhyme put it:

> *Sugar and spice and everything nice,*
> *That's what little girls are made of, made of*
> *That's what little girls are made of.*
>
> *Snips and snails and puppy dog tails,*
> *That's what little boys are made of, made of,*
> *That's what little boys are made of.*

From childhood on, we've been given the cues that influence our attitudes toward the opposite sex. Whether we complain about being stereotyped, or cry "foul" when it comes to equal treatment of the sexes, much of our ability to deal smoothly with each other is really based on learned expectations.

What happens when those expectations are abruptly changed? Part of the discontent expressed in our interviews is that either the rules governing male/female behavior are unclear or no one pays attention to them anymore. Although one might label the biblical story of Samson and Delilah as "sexist" in its stereotypes, nonetheless it depicts clearly the lines of acceptable warfare between the sexes. Samson's power is based on his strength as a warrior; Delilah overcomes him first with her beauty, which lays him open to trust, and second with her wiles. She pries the secret of his strength from him, then drugs him, and uses her knowledge to render him helpless against his enemies. Not a nice lady perhaps, but as a patriot, battling for her country—Mata Hari of the Philistines—she is using a legitimate strategy against brute strength.

There used to be certain implicit rules in the battle of the sexes. In the past it was assumed that females would primarily use the weapons of psychological warfare, which included flattery, cajoling, and the withholding of affection. In addition, some would argue that in the past a woman held the most powerful tools of all for persuasion, the keys to the kitchen and the bedroom. They would contend that her economic dependence was small in comparison to her power, that she knew how to get what she wanted and usually did.

When women move into the realm of males, governed by male rules, and refuse to relinquish their female weapons, they are perceived by men as taking unfair advantage—using muscle plus coquetry. It is a little like bringing a pistol *and* a saber to the duel. Since men cannot easily use female weapons to restore the balance, they see themselves as treated unfairly. One of the most common protests from men concerning women today is, "They can't have it both ways!"

Given changing rules for behavior, intimate relationships become increasingly risky. No one can hurt us as much as those who know us best, especially by taking advantage of our soft spots and hot buttons. So how do you protect yourself? One solution is to make sure no one gets close enough to deal a mortal blow. But another is to play by the Marquis of Queensbury rules for intimacy: No hitting below the belt, and no punching in the clinches.

Women need to understand that if they choose to operate

by male values, then they must be consistent; no batting your eyes in the boardroom.

Armageddon—The Reality of AIDS

Singles had just weathered the herpes storm when AIDS appeared. An early reaction of some to initial press reports of AIDS was, "Homosexuals are killing each other, so what?" But soon other high-risk groups and behaviors were identified, and it didn't take long for everyone to figure out that the disease could spread to the heterosexual population as well. The new axiom became, "Remember, when you have sex, it's not just with one person, but with all the people they've had sex with, too."

For many, putting the brakes on the so-called sexual revolution was a relief—for too many, sex had slipped out of control and no one knew how to reverse it.

Max, a thirty-four-year-old finance director, told us, "At least AIDS took the pressure off. You don't have the feeling anymore that you've got to go to bed with anyone and everyone."

Donna, a twenty-seven-year-old secretary, reported, "In a way I'm glad. I heard a guy talking by the coffee machine the other day; I think he was giving someone advice, and you know what he said? 'Women vary a lot in their sex performance. If you go out with a dud, you're going to have a dud time.' It's pretty disgusting if that's the way guys are thinking about it."

A thirty-three-year-old filmmaker remarked, "It was all such a media hype—liberated sex. I was at a women's college and no matter what you went to the health center for, a broken finger or a sprained knee, the first question they asked was if you were pregnant. It was considered very 'in' to talk about your method of 'protection.' Now with AIDS, I suppose the talk is all about condoms. Not very much changes."

Debra, a thirty-one-year-old interior decorator, commented, "Look, I'm not a religious fanatic, but I'm sure the big AIDS scare is God's way of saying, 'Hey, all the sex stuff has got to go.' I don't know anyone who's taking it lightly."

Whether or not the reality of AIDS will have any long-term effect on the sexual behavior of homosexuals is still unknown. But safe sex and/or abstinence will have an extended effect only if it becomes an extended practice. Evidence shows for any behavior change—whether it is smoking, diet, or use of birth control—what individuals report as their intended behavior frequently has little relationship to what they actually do.

For heterosexuals, AIDS is proving to have enough of a social effect that TV writers have been instructed to include "safer sex" concepts in even their most steamy scenes, to make them believable. This has created a certain dilemma in programs that rely more on heavy breathing than on plot. A recent bedroom fantasy assumed a Monty Python flair when the femme fatale murmured to the good-looking guy who had just dropped by that the condoms were on the bedside table and that she would join him there in a few minutes. Then, slithering onto the bed, she whispered sexily, "It's okay. I'm prepared."

Unfortunately, such TV depictions lend a comic air to a deadly serious problem. One man compared AIDS to a mine field: "It's like seeing gold lying on the ground, almost within your reach, but if you rush in to get it, you can wind up dead. I've stopped sleeping with anyone. Nothing is worth that kind of risk."

A twenty-seven-year-old woman told us, "People can talk about safe sex all they want. The fact is, the only protection against AIDS or anything else is to make sure the person you sleep with doesn't have it. What makes anyone think a condom is going to protect you from someone who's got AIDS?"

There has been growing interest in dating organizations

that supposedly screen for AIDS, but it is unlikely they will prove to be any more popular than other dating clubs. A major objection is that joining such a club implies the end goal is going to bed with members. In the practical realm, it is argued such a club cannot guarantee that a member is really "clean" or that he or she will stay that way.

The overall effect of AIDS and other sexually transmitted diseases (STDs) has been a major shift toward a cautionary climate of sexual behavior that is reminiscent of the fifties. Embodied in the trend toward responsible sex is renewed awareness that the sexual act has very concrete consequences, a concept that had nearly disappeared with the security of the pill. But one major difference today is knowing that sexual consequences, in the form of disease, will be felt equally by men and women. This was not the case in the fifties, when the negative effects of sex were experienced primarily by women, in the form of unwanted pregnancy.

One result of the AIDS threat is that potential partners must now be soberly considered as individuals with a complex of habits and personal history. The days of casual sex are gone for all but the most reckless. Today, getting to know a potential sexual partner in advance is the only reasonable alternative to demanding complete medical records.

AIDS, herpes, and other STDs have had two major consequences for singles: First, for those who do not wish to engage in sexual behavior, the pressure is off. There is now a clear, socially acceptable, excuse to abstain. Second, for those seeking partners, the lure of the one-night stand has been replaced by "responsible sex." This means increased chances of being cherished for who you are, rather than for your bedside manner.

Putting It Back Together

Throughout our interviews we heard, underlying even the most flippant remarks, a certain regret (beyond the AIDS

72

fear). Neither men nor women were very happy with the present state of "progress" that has fostered revolving-door relationships and guerrilla tactics between the sexes.

But there was also a clear sense that things are beginning to change. We began to hear over and over, an expressed preference for serious, permanent, relationships.

Ted, a thirty-seven-year-old health club manager, told us, "I think we're experiencing a mellowing-out effect. People can settle down and think about what they really want. Nothing's going to put an end to sex. But I think we were all getting a little tired of the way things were going."

In a recent magazine article one psychologist suggested the problem with relationships today is that "they need more romance." Apparently the idea is catching on. A New York attorney recently launched a service to write monthly love letters to the person of your choice ("mushy but no sex"), and is doing quite well. Other services are springing up that consult on various aspects of providing the perfect romantic setting, once again, with the emphasis on *romance*, not sex.

Coupled with a renewed emphasis on the romantic is the notion of "rational love." However, there seems to be some confusion over the difference between "rational" and "romantic." An article in *Cosmopolitan* noted, "These days the rational lover is most often a reformed romantic who has overdosed on sexual adventurism and rediscovered the joys of committed love." In this context, "romantic" is treated as a synonym for lack of sexual restraint, while "rational" describes a return to the use of old-fashioned common sense in relationships.

Others view the new trend as a merging of the rational with the romantic, and believe it is shaping up as the love of the future. Among those we interviewed, the swing of the pendulum is clearly toward more traditional, conservative values.

Barbara, a forty-three-year-old English professor, told us, "I want integrity, honesty, and being friends. My standards have changed; in my first marriage I was never able to hash things out, to really talk things over. I would want to be able to do that with someone now. Communication is really important."

A thirty-six-year-old office manager observed, "Among the women I knew there really is a change. Everyone is looking for more than sex for the fun of it, but men are getting more that way too. People are talking about quality rather than quantity, and that is a change."

Jennie, a twenty-nine-year-old mathematician, told us, "Permanence is on everyone's mind these days. Most of my friends definitely want marriage, whether they say it or not. A friend will tell you she's never going to get married and then a few months later you get a wedding invitation."

Bruce, a thirty-one-year-old sports writer, summed up the sentiments of many when he told us, "It's more important to be friends and to be compatible than to be in love. More and more people are looking for friends first, lovers later."

The trend toward more conservative behavior in relationships was first observed among college students. When the sexual revolution swept the campuses in the late sixties, the question was: Would future college students become free-swinging libertines? As results from the December 1984 "*Newsweek* On-Campus Poll" demonstrated, definitely not. According to the poll, the majority of students were resoundingly against casual sex, for fidelity in marriage, and split on the question of living together. Apparently students had observed the effects of the sexual revolution on the generation that preceded them, and decided to make this one case where they would, indeed, learn from their "elders."

Rules for Intimacy

After listening to the opinions and experiences of hundreds of single men and women trying to find intimate, loving, relationships, this is our simple, three-step outline for success.

74

Know What You Want   We thought this was the obvious first step, until people told us, "I never really thought about it," "I sort of play it by ear," "I usually wait and see." For many activities, a "go with the flow" approach creates opportunity, and is just plain fun. Not so when it comes to intimacy.

We recommend that you take a thoughtful, self-inventory of your personal value system, and decide the limits of behavior you wish to engage in. What are you most comfortable with? If you find that you "do," rather than "don't," will you hate yourself in the morning? The "do" may apply to anything from a simple kiss to an overnight. Don't wait for a pressure situation to develop before you decide. Consider this exercise a little like a fire drill. The time to find the exit is *before* the flames are lapping at your feet.

Going Public   Our second rule is to be up-front. Let her/ him know your limits. It isn't fair to invite someone to the airport without letting the person know whether it's for a plane ride or a parachute jump. Your date needs some preparation, too.

There are, of course, tactful ways to do this. You do not have to introduce yourself with, "Hi. My name's John and I don't sleep with anyone." People who are forthright about letting others know their limits report that the response is generally positive. But even in today's climate of assumed sexual sophistication, many find it easier to engage in sex than to talk about it. Those who have cultivated the fine art of routinely communicating their limits have suggested the following methods:

• It's not me, it's my friend: This tactic uses the example of a real or mythical friend to get the point across. "My pal Gus does X or Y, and I think that's a pretty good (or terrible) idea."

• It was in the paper: This approach uses a current news item as an opening to convey your preferences. You've just read a report on growing celibacy in the United States and could really understand why people were doing that (or that it was the weirdest thing you had ever heard).

• The direct approach: This involves disclosing information about yourself with a mild editorial note. You're fresh from a miserable relationship, and find yourself favoring the slow and easy approach. Or your last relationship was so great you're looking for the same thing with someone new.

But remember, the whole point of being up-front is to remove some of the stress and uncertainty from relationships. These suggestions are recommended only to the degree that they accomplish this for you, personally.

Sticking to Your Guns Once you've defined the limits of your behavior for yourself, consider them chiseled in stone. Regardless of the moonlight moment or that extra glass of champagne, remind yourself no "on the spot" renegotiation is permitted.

If you are convinced he/she is that special person you've been searching for, and you would like to redefine your behavior accordingly, fine. But do it in the hard light of day, when that person is nowhere in sight, and you have both the time and quiet to rethink your position.

Not only will these rules for intimacy help you to translate into rational that behavior which often is not, but most of all they will allow you to keep in tact a very precious commodity—your self-esteem.

One last note If you intend physical intimacy to be a part of your relationship, you've got to talk about AIDS. If you are thinking "easier said than done," you're right; but it's a topic that must be covered.

5

Methods and Madness

You walk into a crowded room—on the other side, standing alone, is someone who captures your attention. Your eyes meet. You move through the crowd toward each other. You begin to talk, softly, eagerly. The hour grows late, but neither of you notices. The hostess frowns—you smile at each other and leave together, laughing. This is the magic night of your dreams. This is the night you have met your one true love.

There is nothing wrong with the dream, except the disappointment that it almost never happens. Worse yet, to the degree that the dream differs from reality, it can be painful. "Don't get your hopes too high" is the common cautionary note. Today that piece of advice is more appropriate than ever before. Why? Because today the gap between the dream and the reality has become akin to the distance between Earth and Pluto.

Ten or fifteen years ago the dream meeting (eyes across a crowded room) was in reality an awkward encounter at the school dance in the gym, or a contrived introduction to the cute girl or guy who passed you in the halls. Nothing too dramatic, or too threatening. Today, the reality is all too often a hand on your knee five minutes after meeting at the bar, or waiting at some coffee shop for the latest response to your singles ad— hoping for the spectacular, relieved with the presentable.

Making Up Your Own Rules

From a distance, today's dating scene may look free, sophisticated, and like fun. There are few rules to inhibit; the norms for behavior are whatever will be tolerated. It's an unending *Where the Boys Are* or *Bachelor Party Revisited*. So how come most of the people on the dating scene describe it as a fate second only to walking on hot coals?

Unfortunately, like the stuff of many fantasies, the myth of the utopian "anything goes" date withers under examination in the harsh light of day. For most, the absence of rules is not fun—a fact most of us hate to admit. From the first time someone told us as kids, "Eat your carrots or you don't get any dessert," achieving adulthood meant the day would come when we could say, "Forget the carrots, dammit, I'm eating the dessert." Unfortunately (for the kid in us), by the time that day came, most of us had heard enough about cellulose and related evils to not only eat the carrots, but often to skip the dessert as well.

The point is, rules generally have a very useful function. In the case of dating, they delineate limits, and it is within that framework of limits that shared expectations exist. This means you can measure your preferences and behavior against some sort of impartial yardstick. In this case, general social expectations. An incident a few years ago involved a young woman on a blind date, arranged by her mother, through his mother. The young woman reported the man was a mother's dream—just completing medical school, respectable family, no attachments. The young man was invited over for dinner; afterward they all gathered in the living room to watch TV. Her brother, sitting next to the date, slipped off his shoes to be comfortable. The date, who enjoyed practical jokes, leaned over, whipped out his lighter, and lit her brother's socks on fire! "And he thought it was hilarious," she said. "Even my mother was ready to throw him out." Obviously this was a case where social expectations were not shared. But at least the standards were clear enough to those present that the date's behavior was unanimously defined as intolerable.

What happens when the standards are not clear? When

the expectations are not shared? Or worse yet, what if they keep changing—if expectations become person-specific because there is so much variety in individual standards that they cannot be covered by a single set of rules?

Using the burning socks as an example may at first seem a bit ridiculous; certainly there is no social climate that would encourage flaming footwear. But try another scenario. What if the young woman has just finished dinner at his house, and they are sitting around the living room with two or three of his friends. He lights one of his friend's socks on fire and they all begin to double up with laughter. She may begin to wonder if there is something wrong with *her* sense of humor.

Dating without rules is a little like that. Without the shared yardstick, the atmosphere is predominantly one of uncertainty. The uncertainty itself is not only unnerving, but contributes to an adversarial climate. Cliff, a thirty-five-year-old history professor, described his reaction to his last few dates. "I'm about ready to give up," he told us. "You just don't know what women want. I spent fifty bucks the last time I took a girl out for a few drinks. I thought we had a pretty good time. But when I called her a week later, she was like an iceberg. It turned out I should have called her the next day or so to tell her what a great time I had! There's really something screwy about that. I spend the money and I'm supposed to reassure her besides?"

Some men told us they intentionally avoid calling too soon after a date so they won't appear too eager or, worse yet, "needy." Women, on the other hand, resent the lack of feedback or reinforcement. A thirty-two-year-old interior designer complained, "Men still have the upper hand. Sure it's okay to call him, but what are you going to say? 'This is a quiz: Did you have a good time last night? How good?' I don't want to start falling for someone and then find out I misread the signals."

The need to protect one's self-esteem on the dating scene

was expressed throughout the interviews. It appears that without well-defined rules, you have to work even harder to make sure your flight on the wings of romance doesn't end in a crash landing.

In the past, dating was less complex, and often less stressful, because men and women could rely on certain outward signs that had the same meaning for both. For example:

- If she kissed on the first date, she was easy.

- If he asked you out more than two weekends in a row, it was serious.

- Dating exclusively (going steady) was the first step toward engagement.

The rules provided a clear shorthand for individual intentions; but such rules are only possible when there is some consensus on the meaning of behavior, based on shared cultural norms.

In the Good Old Days

When dating first became popular among college students after World War I, it was intended as a period of freedom to explore the field of eligibles. It was the first step over the threshold toward acknowledging the opposite sex and testing the waters of preference prior to making a commitment to one person in marriage.

Parents were well aware of this. Dating became an expectation; part of the growing-up process. More than one mom worried when the phone never rang for her daughter or when her son showed less interest in girls than in his science project. Until recent times, dating was chiefly a youthful enterprise, engaged in while candidates were most plentiful, during the years of education and job training. It was not unusual for colleges to be treated as hunting grounds for husbands, both by women and by their parents. It should be added that this came as no surprise to college men, who also expected to find mates by the time they graduated.

With so many men and women of the same age dating at the same time, it is not surprising that expectations were similar. In addition, their dating was of a more public nature. A major feature of dating in high school and college was the importance of one's peers. Group opinion about your date frequently dictated your feelings: If the guys in your crowd all thought she was a dog, it's unlikely you would date her more than once. By the same token, if your sorority sisters pronounced him a geek, chances are your feelings would rapidly cool. This involvement of one's peers tended to make dating in high school and college something of a group function, further adding to its stability.

Peer groups also functioned as great teachers. They taught us to internalize certain values and to pronounce judgment, not only on the behavior of others, but on our own behavior as well. The problem is, as more people chose to remain single after leaving the influence of peer groups, they lost a valuable social barometer to aid in judgments about individuals and dating behavior.

Shame on You—The Girl Who Sent Herself a Valentine

In chapter 1 we discussed the structural changes that make it more difficult for singles to find each other today. But it is equally important to realize that the structure itself has an impact on the development of the individual's sense of what's okay.

When the individual date was in some respect a group effort, one had the benefit of constant feedback to help sort out and monitor feelings. That kind of social mirror is less common as the privacy of adulthood prevents one from telling all. Along with the move toward privacy is the scarcity of interested adult listeners to help you interpret what a date's behavior means. Now, instead of an eager group of ready listeners to advise, listen, and compare notes, as in your student days, you've got to figure it out for yourself.

But there is another wrinkle. When you were in high school or college, your desirability as a dating partner affected your status in the group. Choices in dating operated as a sort of public voting system. The "big men on campus" or the most popular girls were also those most sought after as dates. This method of establishing a pecking order is so well understood by the participants that college men and women often report they will refuse a date rather than be seen with someone they consider a social liability, and that they often refuse last-minute invitations to avoid the appearance of being too available.

But there is a limit to what you can do to enhance your own image. There was a girl in high school once who was not very popular. On Valentine's Day she came to school with a beautiful, expensive-looking valentine and told everyone it had been sent to her by a secret admirer. Later it came out that she had sent the valentine to herself. She could not have been more totally ostracized if she had committed a murder. Even after graduation it was the main thing people remembered about her: She was the girl who had sent herself a valentine.

What was so terrible about that? The crime was not one of loneliness or lack of popularity, but one of cheating, in this case fooling classmates into believing she had something she did not—a secret admirer. It was in the same category as claiming your father was a millionaire, or Elvis Presley was your uncle—a way of fixing the popularity vote.

The sense of failure over not being chosen, or of needing help in finding someone, has a long history associated with varying degrees of humiliation. Your aunt fixes you up with your beautiful cousin because you don't have a date for the school prom and you slink around the whole evening hoping you won't have to introduce her to anyone. Or your mother arranges for her tennis partner's son to escort you to the Christmas dance and you spend half the night worrying over what your friends will think.

Those feelings do not automatically disappear when you reach twenty-five, or thirty-five, or forty-two. They linger, and become especially problematic in today's climate where the responsibility for locating dating partners has shifted primarily to the individual. Just when you most need to develop your own strategies for seeking someone, you are still carrying around the high school message that says there is something vaguely shameful about trying to find someone yourself, rather than waiting to be chosen. To complicate matters, as soon as you admit you are actively trying to find someone, your self-esteem is on the line.

Yet despite all of the problems, singles *are* carrying on their own search, and devising new strategies to find each other. In fact, one of the most powerful testimonies to the strength of the need for intimacy is the extent to which singles are willing to go to try to satisfy that need, despite both the internal and external roadblocks.

The Fixer-Uppers—Informal Matchmakers

The intermediate step between relying on institutions and finding someone yourself is to depend on the efforts of friends. It often worked well in school situations. Studies of college-aged daters show some groups of girlfriends reported using an exchange of introductions to date whole fraternities, person by person. When spring came, and their pool was used up, they would start on a new fraternity—one friend dating one member, and introducing her girlfriends to the others. But even then, dating was, in a sense, supported by the school setting, which provided large numbers of eligibles to begin with.

Singles who have left the educational setting behind report

that friends are no longer very useful in helping them find someone. This is due to several factors, one of which is the reluctance of singles to ask their friends for help. From this group a typical comment was, "I don't ask them to fix me up because I don't want my friends to know I'm lonely, desperate; there's a stigma to it."

But those who have asked haven't fared much better. A mid-thirties bachelor told us, "My friends never pick the right kind of woman for me. Either they don't really know me, or they tend to pair people up just to have an even number." A forty-three-year-old woman remarked, "The men they fix me up with. I'm really disappointed. The last guy had a serious drinking problem. She didn't know about it, but then you wonder how much she knew about him in general."

The issue of how safe you can feel with your friends' selections came up over and over. Lisa, a thirty-one-year-old legal assistant, described her one and only blind date: "I had someone fix me up once. She kept telling me this guy had a Corvette. We went to a movie and he spent the whole time in the bathroom. Afterward we went to my apartment and he just lunged at me. I said, 'You get the hell out of here,' and that was that. I'll never let her fix me up again."

Both men and women were surprised and disappointed at the inability of friends to be much help in their dating efforts. We heard the same sort of complaints about friends from almost everyone we interviewed. Part of the problem is obvious: You are usually trying to enlist the aid of *married friends*, since unmarrieds are keeping their little black books under wraps. Because married friends do not usually have many single friends, they begin their attempts at matchmaking with a much smaller pool. Often the single friends they do have are former couples now in the midst of a divorce, which does not make them the best dating candidates.

Also, women generally ask other women to help them find someone. The approach of these friends is usually to ask

their husbands if there are any unattached men at the office
—hardly the type of sorting process that allows for a calculated match.

However, even if your friends have access to a variety of
singles, you may be surprised at the choices they make for
you. Singles expressed dismay at some of the differences in
evaluation of potential partners between themselves and
their friends. But when one considers that their friends have
been involved in very different life-styles, it seems reasonable
to expect differences in expectations and values as well. The
married man who thinks his bachelor friend will be thrilled
over the office manager with the sunny personality, in spite
of the few extra pounds she carries, is basing his judgment
on a twenty-four-hour-a-day living situation. By the same
token, a married woman may place special value on the
"good father" potential of the otherwise ordinary young
man she introduces to her friend.

This doesn't mean friends should be totally ruled out as
possible matchmakers, but it does mean you should not rely
on them as a major source of social connections. The best
approach is to use the resources at your disposal, but not to
view any as an all-or-nothing proposition. We found that
people who did not pin their hopes on any single meeting,
and who thought of each introduction as broadening their
social network, were the same ones who were most sought
after, and usually did not stay single for long.

If You Can't Find It in the Yellow Pages— Advertise

Most major cities have a weekly paper devoted primarily
to the in crowd with disposable income, and filled with suggestions on how to dispose of it: the most interesting restaurants, foreign and domestic films, up-coming events, art
openings, etc. But whether it's *The Reader, The Weekly, The
Uptowner, The Downtowner, The Weekender,* or *The Sub-*

urbanite, whether in L.A., Chicago, New York, Denver, Minneapolis, or D.C., these papers contain a section avidly read by virtually every unattached reader: the personal ads.

The personals, which have become one of the most popular and innovative ways for postcollege singles to meet, were a natural offshoot of an age of rapid communication, spawned in the spirit of "You can find it in the yellow pages," or if you can't find it, "Advertise, advertise, advertise!"

Just a few years ago, the personals were most typically the stuff of X-rated fantasies or thinly veiled covers for prostitution. But once singles discovered these ads could function as a legitimate meeting ground, they have been steadily gaining in respectability and popularity.

No one is sure how many thousands of letters in response to personal ads find their way to newspaper and magazine mailrooms each month, but a few years ago *New York Magazine* estimated its share alone at six thousand per week.

Why their tremendous popularity? In discussing individual strategies for meeting and dating, both men and women told us they feel least threatened using methods over which they feel they have most control. In its initial stage, the personal ad provides a certain degree of anonymity. Once you place an ad or answer one, you still have a telephone call during which you can gather information, assess, and ultimately choose whether you still want to meet. The key factor with the personals is the degree to which you retain your veto power.

Reasons for using the personals are almost as varied as the people themselves. Some share the view of the young businessman who has placed ads because "There's a different attitude about the ads [from other ways of meeting]— they're kind of hip." Others share the attitude of the investment counselor about to turn forty who told us, "My boyfriend just moved out; I don't know many people in this town. What have I got to lose?"

Some singles answer the personals "just for fun." A thirty-five-year-old woman working on her Ph.D. in psychology told us, "I don't have time for a personal relationship just now, but every now and then I'll read the ads and answer five or six of them. Usually I get a few calls. I'll go out with them once or twice. It's been fun. Just about the level of commitment I need right now."

Others look upon the ads as a last resort. A fifty-three-year-old widower told us, "I never thought I'd put in an ad, but I just didn't know what else to do. During the time my wife was ill, I lost touch with our friends. After she was gone it was like starting over again. I think the ads are great. I've met some really nice women."

People place ads because they are bored, lonely, desperate, or simply too busy to try other methods. For some it is a lark, and for others it's serious business. An advertising manager told us, "My favorite aunt is fifty-two. On her last birthday, I ran a singles ad for her. She got six or seven responses and went out with three of them. She still sees this one guy. It was great for her."

A thirty-four-year-old male health club operator was less enthused: "I put in an ad once. I got one response. I called her up. She sounded okay on the phone, but when I met her she was about a hundred pounds overweight. I couldn't believe it. My ad said slim, and that I wanted someone athletic like myself. It was a workout for this woman to get in and out of a chair."

A thirty-two-year-old female nutritionist remarked, "I've answered half a dozen of those ads, but I never once had anyone call me. They must get so many people writing. They probably only pick out a couple of the best ones. I spend all that time—it takes time to answer an ad, you know—and never hear a thing. That's discouraging."

One advantage to placing an ad yourself is that the responses are sent to you; it is up to you to pick and choose among them, and to pick the time you want to call. Most per-

sonal ads work in a similar way: You write a letter of response (including your telephone number) to the ad of your
choice and place it in a sealed envelope with the advertiser's
number on the corner. You put that envelope into a larger
one (sometimes with a handling fee—usually a few dollars),
which is sent directly to the magazine or newspaper. Responses are forwarded to the person who placed the ad.

The number of responses to an ad varies enormously,
from as few as one or two to the three hundred reported by
a Manhattan surgeon who was deluged by *mothers* writing
to say they had an eligible daughter and would love having a
doctor in the family.

Men place more ads than women do, but women tend to
get more responses. The average for the women we interviewed was about thirty. One woman told us she had received twenty responses, but that her neighbor, who had
placed a later ad with similar wording, had received sixty.

The only person we spoke with who reported getting absolutely no responses to his ad was a forty-three-year-old
computer scientist who wrote in his ad that he was looking
for a woman who was a "highly intelligent, computer liter-
ate cross between Dolly Parton and Gloria Steinem."

We talked with both men and women who reported they
received so many responses to their ads that by the time they
were able to answer them, they thought too much time had
elapsed. A twenty-eight-year-old administrative secretary
told us, "I didn't think I would get so many responses, and
they all sound like people I would enjoy meeting. But I had
no idea it could be so much work. I just don't have time to
go out more than two or three times a week, which means I
can only call about a dozen people in a month, at best. It
means you have to really pick and choose."

One shy forty-nine-year-old told us he has been carrying
around a letter he received in response to an ad three months
ago. "I still want to call her," he said. "She wrote a wonderful letter; she sounds like the perfect person for me, but the
more time that goes by, the harder it gets."

The success of ads and the number of responses depend primarily on what you have to say, although, like shopping for anything else, they are governed to some degree by seasonal variations. There is an upswing in ad activity in the fall, when people are contemplating a long cold winter alone, and there is usually a pre–Valentine's Day surge of activity when the stores are filled with red paper hearts and displays of cards for your one true love.

Ad content varies enormously. According to one avid reader, "The problem is, if you read the ads everyone is slim, attractive, likes to walk in the woods, have a quiet evening in front of the fireplace, and go to concerts. So what else is new?"

His observation was not far off. One informal computer content analysis created a composite of the personal ads from several newspapers. The results showed that advertisers were all "slim, intelligent, music lovers, who, when they aren't sipping wine in front of the fireplace, love to walk in the woods."

There was general agreement that the best ads are the most specific ones. In fact, the value of a good ad is such that several businesses have sprung up to help individuals write the ad that captures their special qualities. The idea is that very specific ads may attract fewer responses, but because they screen people according to your preferences, in the long run they will save you both time and disappointment. One ad writer told us, "There are a lot of people placing ads out there. You need to be unique—I favor anything that sets you apart, short of lying."

Specific ads may be primarily factual or attempt to capture an attitude: "Blond vegetarian would like to meet thoughtful, organized, agile, childhearted woman, 25–40, for forest walks, icicle dueling, reading out loud, easy silences, radiance, Taoist romance."

Some ads are practical and straightforward: "Divorced white male, 45, active engineer, enjoys kids, TV, movies, sports, some opera, church. Raising teenage daughter, able to compromise."

Some ads try an offbeat approach: "Male Jerk Wants Chick
—insecure, insensitive, white male. Loves sitting, sleeping,
drinking beer, and watching TV. Hates travel, reading, exercise, the arts, and anything new. Seeks excheerleader to spend
romantic nights at my home cleaning and doing laundry."

Singles find some ads intimidating. We wonder how many
women responded to the following: "Male, 29, very handsome, very athletic, and very well built, successful professional with positive view on life, seeks exceptionally cute
personable woman 21–30 with outstanding characteristics,
financial independence, traditional values, college degree,
and curvaceous petite figure under five feet four."

Or how many replies were received by the self-described
"Millionaire intellectual over forty seeking warm beautiful
woman who appreciates creative, thoughtful vegetarian."

Sometimes the ad prompts more curiosity about the advertiser than anything else: "Incurable romantic looking for very
special man 28–38. Good build, good-looking, in good shape.
No liars, baldies, or potbellies." Or: "Attention queen-size
ladies who are single and weigh 250 pounds or more. Age is
unimportant. Here is a single gentleman who needs you."

For some, the ads have met with mixed success. A thirty-
six-year-old commercial artist told us, "Two years ago I put
in an ad and wound up dating a woman for six months. She
was intelligent, down to earth, and moneyed. After we broke
up I tried the ads again, but I'm having a run of bad luck."

For others, placing ads has not only been disappointing,
but expensive. An L.A. newspaper recently quoted a twenty-
seven-year-old insurance adjuster as saying, "I've spent a
thousand dollars on personal ads this year and I've met
nearly 150 women. Two, maybe three, were worth asking
out twice."

But there is a good chance that if your ad is realistic and
clear in its expectations, it will attract your dream person, as
it has for some. Mac is thirty-one, good-looking, with a Brit-
ish accent and a Woody Allen sense of humor. When we

interviewed him he had been in the Chicago area for six months as sales rep for a London-based company. He considers the personals an ideal way to meet people: "The first thing I did when I got here was put an ad in one of those papers. Lots of girls answered. The first one I met, I'm still dating. She's fantastic." He described their first meeting as a memorable one. "We got arrested. We were having such a good time, and it was a hot night. We decided to go skinny-dipping, and they nabbed us, down to the station and everything. She was so good-humored about the whole thing. Maybe that's why we're still together. I never called any of the other girls."

Successful Advertising—Rules for the Personals

The personal ads have worked for people in all age ranges. In fact, they have been especially effective for the older crowd. For them, the key seems to be candidness, attention to detail, seriousness about wanting to find someone, and willingness to accept less than perfection.

An ad will be most effective if you carefully consider the best publication for you. Apart from local newspapers, there are local and national clubs and magazines that publish personals for people who share common interests. For example, there are book club personals for bibliophiles and running club personals for the fleet-footed.

Writing an ad is not easy. One person complained, "It's like trying to quantify your personality." But easy or not, for many it has been worth the trouble. If you are thinking of placing an ad of your own, there are a few basic rules to observe.

Be informative Ask yourself, if there were only three things you could say about yourself, what would they be? Here the key is to be both specific and relevant. Answers like "loves horses," "cooks Italian," "prefers mystery novels to TV," "is trying to learn French," "builds bird condos," all give some specific information about you. Compare that to "Divorced male, 44, looking for friends in all the wrong places. Needs to change that. Want to help?"

Avoid listing vague characteristics Some descriptions may have different meanings for different people, as in the following ad: "Seeks woman who is not passive or overbearing, knows what she wants for a relationship. Important commonalities: independence, communication, courage, intelligence..." Compare this ad to one of our favorites: "Cicero wrote, 'Love is the attempt to form a friendship inspired by beauty.' I am a successful nonfiction writer looking for an equally exciting, successful man."

Don't ask for a photo Most people will not send one anyway, and even some very attractive people may be intimidated by the emphasis on physical appearance. A pretty thirty-two-year-old blonde told us, "I wouldn't have the nerve to answer one of those ads—I couldn't meet their expectations." Another woman commented, "Thank goodness I've never sent a photo. I would think that's why they didn't call."

Safety First

Before you place or answer an ad, be sure you know the rules for protecting yourself. According to one woman, "I could never put in an ad. I would be scared to death." A sales manager remarked, concerning the ads, "There's no question about it. A woman is taking a chance. If Jack the Ripper were around today he'd put an ad in the personals."

We disagree. In all of our interviews not one person who used the ads reported any problems of being frightened or of encountering aggressiveness in their meetings. But this may be partly because singles follow a strict set of rules for these meetings, which are:

- Never allow the person to come to your home for a first meeting.

- Always meet in a public place, preferably for lunch or coffee.

- Always provide your own transportation.

- Keep the first meeting short. This rule is not so much for safety as a "bail out" measure. If you can't stand each other, the agony will at least be limited. If it's sheer magic, you can arrange to get together soon enough.

At Your Service—What Dating Bureaus Offer

While the personal ads have been growing in popularity over the past few years, there has also been a dramatic rise in the activity of dating bureaus. We see their advertisements everywhere:

THE NETWORK	fun for everyone, discover a whole new world of adventure, excitement, romance (confidential, legitimate, fast).
SINGLES NETWORK	the contemporary dating service. If Cupid can't find your number, call us.
SPECIAL SINGLES	mature singles, all 40 to 80; special singles, all handicapped; special singles, all with herpes.

What do the dating services offer? One service, Matchmate, advertises "personal interviews, personal matching, video and photo dating, professional photos, personality analysis, handwriting analysis, astro-romance (25-page computer compatability analyzation), men and women of all ages and professions, twenty-four-hour answering service." Some dating services send a representative to your home to interview you in your native habitat, the idea being that they can tell more about you in your own environment, and thus select a better match. Some conduct in-depth interviews to determine your preferences; others simply have you fill out a form. Prices vary from a twenty-five-dollar registration fee to several hundred dollars and a several month commitment. What do you get for your money? Most of the more expensive services guarantee a minimum number of contacts per month. When someone appears compatible, they will be given your telephone number and told to call you. It is up to you to decide if you want to make a contact.

How effective are dating services in bringing people together? When singles shifted their discussion from the personals to dating services, there was more skepticism and discomfort. A twenty-eight-year-old physical therapist told us, "When you move to the idea of a dating service it's different. It would be embarrassing to have to resort to that sort of thing. I read the personal ads—some things sound interesting—but to try a service?...If you can't meet someone on your own..." The feeling was echoed in most of our interviews.

Marla, a thirty-one-year-old artist, told us her mother had paid a flat fee for a dating service for her: "I was mortified. They charged a hundred dollars, interviewed me for twenty minutes, and had six guys call me in the next two weeks. We didn't have anything in common, and I never heard from them again. It was the most humiliating thing I ever did."

Paul, a twenty-eight-year-old marketing analyst, reported he had tried a dating service the year before: "Never again. They don't listen to you. I told them there was one type of woman I did not want to date at all, and that's what they sent."

A forty-nine-year-old woman told us she had called a dating service, and they immediately asked her age: "When I told him, the man on the other end said, 'Lady, save your money, we don't have guys that old.' At least he was honest, but I felt pretty discouraged."

One of the problems with dating services, especially in older age ranges, is that they usually do have far more women than men. Since many guarantee a certain number of dates, some services have been accused of sending around men who were not really "eligible," but were paid by the service to help it fulfill its guarantee.

Although, like everyone else, we have seen the ads for dating services and heard testimonials from people who have used them with success, most of the singles we interviewed were reluctant to try them.

Somewhere between the personal ads and the formal dating services, there is an array of loosely constructed organizations aimed at helping men and women meet. "Flirt Alert," "Tail Date," and "Motor Mates" are all singles clubs that depend on driving your way to success. Enrollment means you get an ID in the form of a decal or bumper sticker, and when you see an attractive member, jot down his or her ID and mail it with a letter of introduction to the club office, which forwards it.

Unattached literary buffs can meet through the "Singles Book Lovers Club." A woman who joined told us, "I put in three lines for twenty dollars and heard from only one man. He called me three years after I quit the club, and we had lunch. The problem is distance; I'm in the Midwest, and most of these people are on the East and West Coast."

"Friends, Phones and Fun" is a phone-in service that works this way: You dial a number to phone in your verbal ad, and are charged fifty cents per minute on your phone bill (seventy-five cents if by credit card). If someone wants to meet you they call an operator who screens the call, introduces you by first names, and gets off the line. The charge is $2.50 per call connected.

Most of these specialty services have sprung up in the last few years, testifying to the inadequacy of our present structures to aid in meeting people. As the number of singles continues to increase, and the ways of meeting do not prove satisfactory, we expect to see a refinement of methods and a new legitimacy that will extend to meeting in ways and places we have not yet contemplated.

6

Stepping Out

*F*or unattached singles, the weekend often brings the dreaded Saturday night out (or Friday night, or both). Many singles reported that sometimes they would like to just curl up in front of the TV with a bowl of popcorn and their favorite beverage, but felt an obligation to get out and look —and be looked at.

Jay, a thirty-three-year-old tax consultant told us, "I don't know what it is. I suppose I don't like admitting I don't have anything to do on a Saturday night, but I get the feeling that time is running out, that every evening home is a wasted opportunity. I like to think if I go to enough places and talk to enough women, I'm bound to meet someone. Except that's not true. I've been to a lot of places, a lot of weekends, and I still haven't met anyone."

Brenda, a twenty-nine-year-old interior designer, observed, "I think if you don't at least get out there and try, you haven't anything to gripe about. Sure it's work. Nobody likes to do it. But what are your options?"

Most singles agreed that the process of looking is indeed, surprisingly hard work. A pretty brunette commented, "I thought this stuff was supposed to be fun. But it seems I use up a lot of energy, and I don't feel that great about it."

Mark, a thirty-eight-year-old accountant, described his efforts as "a second full-time job." He added, "I think about it all the time. I'm always working on strategy—where to go and what's the best time to get there. When I walk into a room I give it a quick scan; if I don't like what I see, I leave."

It would be a mistake to think all singles view stepping out as an onerous task. For some, going out is still primarily for the purpose of having fun. According to our interviews, members of this group are in a definite minority; but they are the ones who really do have fun when they go out. Beth, a thirty-four-year-old technical writer, told us, "I love to get all dressed up and go out on a Saturday night. For me it's a real treat just to be somewhere else. I do all my work at home on a word processor; it's a relief to get away from that environment for a change."

Others who genuinely enjoyed stepping out included those who were between relationships and wanted some breathing space before getting immersed in another, and those who were in relationships but occasionally went out by themselves. Why do these people tend to have fun on their nights out while others don't? The answer is a simple matter of motives and expectations.

If a night out means a few glasses of white wine or imported beer, some light conversation, music perhaps, and a heavy dose of people-watching, chances are you won't be disappointed. If, on the other hand, the success of an evening is determined by the degree to which it furthers your ambition of meeting the next significant him or her in your life, most evenings will rate a big zero.

Not only did we find the issue of expectations the best overall predictor of having a fun night out, but the perversity of nature being what it is, those who *least* intended to meet someone were, overall, the *most likely* to do so.

Pull Yourself Together, Charlie Brown

In chapter 1 we talked about the fact that church, school, and family once provided the natural settings for eligible singles to meet. In addition, these structures often extended beyond their formal responsibilities, to provide special programs such as choir, study groups, and community service activities, for which participants were often rewarded with social events that included seasonal parties, sleigh rides, and hay rides.

A basic advantage of all of these activities was that, because their stated goals were learning, service, or rewards for involvement, you could participate enthusiastically and still appear as indifferent as a rock to the idea of meeting someone. You could go to the sleigh ride or Valentine's Day party without being perceived as looking, because you were a member of the group, and these activities were considered group rewards. Of course, in the process, numerous young people suddenly discovered the charm of the girl next door or the boy who used to sit across the aisle in seventh grade, and often found themselves dating and marrying close to home.

Today, it's pretty hard to convey indifference to meeting someone, when that is the stated purpose of so many singles gathering places. Why convey indifference? Isn't that just a bit too coy, if not frankly deceptive? Maybe. But for most it's the much needed protection that enables our fragile egos to publicly risk venturing into unknown waters and returning, for all the world to see, without any fish.

Taking out ads and getting friends to fix you up with an unknown face are ways of meeting people that have a certain strategic advantage, namely, they can be arranged from the comfort of your own living room. The disadvantage is that you do not meet the person until you're already committed to a date, even if it's only coffee after work. To meet someone on your own, to actually see that person in advance of making any time commitment, involves going to the places other singles go.

Phone calls involved in answering the ads or responding to dating services can be nerve-racking, but at least no one can see your nervous flushing or fidgeting across the crackling wires, and if it all becomes too much, there is always the last resort of cutting the connection with a simple click of your finger. Moving from the phone call to "being there" is a giant step.

Singles tell us the difference between writing or calling someone on the phone and meeting face to face is enormous. One man remarked, "It's like the difference between watching the stock car races on film and having your hands on the wheel in the curves."

To those who have never had the experience of entering a room full of single men and women gathered for the express purpose of checking each other out, it is difficult to convey the sheer terror of such a moment. A thirty-two-year-old engineer described attending a singles party advertised in a local paper: "The second you open the door, fifty pairs of eyes are riveted on you; you can just feel yourself being sized up—it takes guts to walk in."

Part of the enormous popularity of the cartoon character Charlie Brown is that he mirrors our foibles. Through one misunderstanding or another, he constantly finds himself in embarrassing situations, eloquently depicted in the telltale line of his mouth and that single expressive phrase, "Good grief." Whether it is an encounter with the little red-haired girl or managing the neighborhood team, he is always just a little out of step. Most of us can tolerate making mistakes, but what we can't live with is looking foolish. We can laugh at it in a comic strip, and even sympathize, but in our own lives, appearing to be foolish has come to be regarded as a fate worse than death.

It is no wonder that singles today shudder at the prospect of going out solely to meet someone. Any adult who owns a TV set has been presented with the scriptwriters' impossible standard for the perfect person: self-possessed, stylish, skilled at social repartee. With this image in mind, men and women are asked to enter the totally unpredictable environment of various singles groups, and to do so with aplomb.

In most of the other avenues of their lives, these singles have things under control. They know what is in and what is not: the most popular cuisine, the latest styles of dress, even the most-watched nighttime soap. For them the issue is not conformity, but that pleasant glow of knowing you've got it all together. Why then ruin a perfectly comfortable self-image by exposing yourself to situations that in their unpredictability are like Russian roulette? The answer is linked to the powerful human need for intimacy. It is in the tenuous hope that the risk will pay off; that in the end, you will find that special someone; that the prize will be worth the effort.

The self-consciousness of frequenting singles spots is aggravated by two major factors. The first is that circumstances have changed faster than our cultural learning has been able to keep pace. While structural changes have dumped the responsibility for finding someone into the lap of the individual, we continue to label individual efforts the same way we did twenty years ago, when structures were doing the job. At that time, and within that structural framework, those who went outside the system to meet on their own were viewed as social misfits. If they were female, it was assumed they were not "nice girls" and could never expect to be brought home to meet the family. If they were males, they were simply "sowing their wild oats," a period of temporary indiscretion that would end with their return to the fold and to the traditional methods of mate selection. Singles today often find they have internalized these old prejudices just when they most need to rely on their own strategies to devise ways of meeting.

The second factor that creates embarrassment for singles is the degree to which their intentions to meet someone are publicly displayed. Most singles spots involve some ego risk, but some are riskier than others. We found a direct relationship between the stated purpose ("this is a bar for meeting singles," or "this is a travel group—members also are single") and the degree of discomfort of the participants. Not surprisingly, the place with the greatest discomfort factor and highest embarrassment level (at admitting you had been there) was the singles bar.

If Nobody Goes to Singles Bars, How Come They're Always Full?

We have heard so much about singles bars in the past few years that it is easy to forget they are a relatively recent phenomenon. When we first began interviewing singles, we thought any discussion of the bar scene could be disposed of in a few paragraphs. We soon discovered that what appeared on the surface to be no more than a quick pickup flesh market for social down-and-outers was far more complex. In many ways the singles bars mirror the larger problems for men and women in a society of changing roles and expectations.

When singles began casting about to replace meeting places lost through structural changes, they soon observed that one place where young men tended to gather, as a sort of natural habitat, was the bar. But the bars were bastions of male supremacy, off-limits to women—at least to those of the "nice girl" variety. The solution was obvious: The bars had to be cleaned up and repackaged to include the fairer sex. Entrepreneurs were quick to comply. They would do anything it took to bring in the droves of men and women ready and willing to patronize whatever place was provided for meeting one another. For businesses, it was a new market: mostly young, moneyed individuals, without family responsibilities, eager to spend the evening buying drinks for the privilege of flirting their way from entry to exit. But there was an additional market—the older, divorced men and women, many new to the singles scene. Members of this group, no longer a statistical anomaly, were more than eager to find ways to meet one another.

Today every major city boasts singles bars that not only cater to different age groups but to a whole spectrum of tastes. Bars range from pure yuppie to blue-collar, with a wide variety that fall somewhere in between.

But despite their proliferation, the bars have not been very successful in establishing themselves as legitimate meeting places for singles (when "success" is defined as more than a one-night stand). One major problem with the bars is that they have not undergone the same process of legitimization that was observed in the personal ads. Part of the reason is that singles bars are up against an established all-male bar tradition. By its nature, the all-male bar was chauvinistic—a haven from the cares of earning a buck and listening to the little woman's endless complaints, a place to escape family pressure, obtain a little relaxation, and compare stories from the trenches, whether corporate or blue-collar.

A by-product of the solidarity of the all-male bar was its stereotypical image of women. Bringing women into the bars did not change that. A thirty-four-year-old orthodontist remarked, "I don't know what it is, but I don't behave the same with women in a bar. It brings out the worst in me." Lucy, a twenty-six-year-old flight attendant, told us, "Men really do act gross in bars. The last time I was home I went with my brother; we're twins and really close. I couldn't believe the way he acted. He stood at the bar with his nose in the air, trying to look like Mr. Wonderful. I wanted to punch him in the stomach."

Judging from interviews and articles throughout the country, despite the variety of patrons, there is an eerie sameness about singles bars. Whether in San Francisco, New York, Detroit, Chicago, or Indianapolis, if you're at a singles bar you're probably munching on buffalo wings or stuffed calamari, drinking wine coolers or imported beer, or sipping a glass of chablis or a rum and Coke. The music is too loud, the men too drunk, the women too animated. Nobody looks like they're having much fun, but they are there.

The bar scene may not exactly be *Paradise Regained*, yet on any Friday or Saturday night the music blares and the bars are full. Why? Who frequents them? According to our firsthand interviews, hardly anyone. Over and over we were told, "I wouldn't be caught dead in one of those places," or, "I went once with a couple of girlfriends, but never again."

A number of singles who insisted they would never try the bars proceeded to give in-depth descriptions of the major singles bars around town—telling us which ones cater to specific groups, and listing the points on which they differ from each other. One man, after enumerating the negatives of going to bars and insisting only losers frequent them, told us, "The last time I went [to a singles bar] I had the worst time of my life. I was trying to talk to this woman and she just walked away."

Both men and women listed a variety of reasons for going to singles bars. Some went "because there's no place else to go." Others told us, "If you're really lonely, at least there are other people around you [in the bar]."

Mitch, a forty-four-year-old policy analyst, remarked, "When I was younger, I did go to bars. But I feel as though I've outgrown them. I get depressed when I go into a bar now—it's too artificial. You look at people's faces, and it's like a caricature of having fun. Everyone feels their success is on the line—their success at being human. You can go a whole night and not have anyone even notice you. You leave feeling incredibly like a piece of crap."

Those who admitted going to bars cited a variety of reasons. For Don, a twenty-nine-year-old musician, it was the music. "There are two ways to look at the bars," he told us. "One is as a pick-up place; the other is just as a place to listen to some music and be with your friends. That's when I have the best time; when I go for the music."

Mandy, a thirty-seven-year-old office manager, told us she has gone to bars a few times with women friends, "Just for something to do. I didn't meet anyone, but I didn't expect to. I went because I was bored."

Steve, an attorney in his early thirties, also cites boredom as a reason for going to the bars. He told us, "It's sort of a last resort—for when I'm not feeling very creative and can't think of anything else to do. I've never met anyone that way, but who knows—there's always a first time."

For Kristie, a thirty-four-year-old dance instructor, the

bars were in response to a divorce. She told us, "I feel like I've gone through my second adolescence. After my divorce I went through a period where I really needed to play. That's what the bars were for me. I thought, 'This is really fun,' laughing and forgetting my problems—a way to get out for a night. But it was only a stage—partly a test. Would men still find me attractive after a marriage and a six-year-old daughter? They did and it was nice. At the time it was just what I needed. But there is definitely a negative connotation of women in bars. I didn't want people to know what I was doing. The bars are full of desperate women and desperate men, and lots and lots of married people."

Only a few of the men and women we interviewed admitted going to bars expressly for a one-night stand. Those who did said it was immediately after a divorce or the breakup of a major relationship. Sam, a forty-seven-year-old opthalmologist, told us, "I just needed a warm body to cling to. It was the first time I had been alone after twenty years of marriage. It was also pre-AIDS—I would never take that kind of a risk today."

Although it is not typical, a few people interviewed told us they have met people in singles bars whom they subsequently dated. Liz, a thirty-year-old CPA, is one of the few people who admitted dating men she meets in the bars. But she also noted they were not exactly what she was looking for: "So far I've met three different guys that way, that I've gone out with; but all they wanted to do was climb into bed. I suppose guys are that way in or out of bars. It doesn't do much for a person's self-image. At least the AIDS scare is putting a brake on that."

Whatever the reasons singles give for going to the bars, most of them admit that deep inside they are always hoping to meet someone. A few of them have. Bill, a fifty-three-year-old engineer, told us he met a woman in a bar with whom he subsequently had a close five-year relationship: "The only problem was she went into treatment for alcoholism and when she dried out, our relationship ended."

Diane, a forty-one-year-old physician's assistant, said that in the past sixteen years she has gone to the same bar nearly every week: "Just so I don't have to sit home by myself. But in all that time I've only met two or three decent men. They're either drinking so much they ask your name and where you work four or five times, or you give them your phone number and they rarely call. It's so plastic and game-playing; but there isn't any place else to go."

Singles were for the most part harsh and unreserved in their criticism of the bars as meeting places. Over and over we listened to descriptions of singles bars that included such terms as "dishonesty," "game-playing," and what one man called "the land of one-night stands and plastic people." Bars were described as having "an inhospitable environment," being "depressing," "expensive," and "a waste of time."

Women complained they were "tired of being approached by people who are nearly drunk." A twenty-eight-year-old market researcher remarked, "Guys that ask you to dance have their hands all over you—half the time they're three sheets to the wind. I don't deserve to be treated that way. Guys are so ready to assume if you're in a bar, you're a pickup."

Men complained about women "banding together" in the bar. According to one, "They get together in these tight little groups; it is almost impossible to approach three or four women at a table to ask one to dance, or to buy a drink for only one of them. It's like trying to get through the circled wagons in the Old West."

Other complaints about the singles bars were: "The music is so loud you can't hear a thing anyone says," "The odds are against anything but a one-night shot," and, "Lying is part of the routine, it's expected—it's part of your survival." One man remarked, "I never tell the truth about myself [in bars]. It's fun to see how preposterous you can be and still be believed. I get a kick out of it."

Mike, a forty-four-year-old restaurateur, agreed that lying

is commonly a part of the bar scene: "I've seen people hand someone their check deposit slip to show they are using their real name. On top of everything else, you never know when the person you're talking to may really be married. I've run into that before. It's pretty simple to just slip your ring off if you want a night out on the town. So how do you protect yourself? I don't want to hurt anyone, but I don't want to get hurt either."

Men and women alike noted the emotional strain involved in frequenting singles bars. For some, the strain lies in issues of rejection; for others it is related to fear. A twenty-nine-year-old secondary school teacher noted, "The few times I went into a bar I got so scared. I was afraid of picking up a jerk—a dangerous one."

Sue, a thirty-eight-year-old dental hygienist, confided that fear of rejection based on age was the real problem for her. She told us she had gone to bars several times with girlfriends: "I looked around at all those women who were younger and prettier, and said to myself, 'I can't compete here.' That's when you really get demoralized."

Singles have their own methods of trying to offset the strain of singles bars. Tim, a forty-three-year-old computer salesman, remarked that self-confidence was at least as important an issue for men as it was for women. He told us, "You go into the men's washroom and see guys looking into the mirror, talking to themselves, trying to psych themselves up, saying things like 'I'm neat, I'm great.' They know self-confidence is important—no one likes a loser. Watch some time when people approach each other. If they don't have pride in themselves, it shows."

Jake, a thirty-three-year-old flight instructor, told us, "Bars work best for the peacock types, the sort who make heads turn. Otherwise you're just lost in the crowd. Nobody notices you; or they're all holding out for something better. You might as well go home."

Throughout our interviews, we noticed that as people described their behavior in bars, many reported that it was not typical of their behavior in other settings. Although individuals reacted in a variety of ways to the bar setting, most of them noted that in one way or another their behavior was changed or exaggerated. Linda, a thirty-four-year-old sales manager, observed, "I go into a bar and I feel myself change. I become angry, cold, defensive. The bar seems to make me act that way—I really can't explain it. Maybe it's just so guys won't hit on me."

Allen, a thirty-seven-year-old physician, says a singles bar makes him feel more interesting and lively, but that it also creates a distortion of his normal behavior: "I'm usually very quiet. For me, it's almost like playacting."

Peter, a thirty-five-year-old landscape architect, claims the bar environment makes him feel "very competitive. I get this feeling if I find someone I'm attracted to, I'd better close in quick, or someone else will get there first. You look around and every guy there is after the same thing. You can't waste any time."

As we examined our interviews on singles bars, we concluded one of the reasons reports on the bars have been so varied, and sometimes conflicting, is that there are several categories of bar-goers. The first and probably the largest group are those who can be classified as one-timers. These are basically non–bar-goers, the people who go into a bar for the first time (perhaps even a second or third), have a miserable time, and resolve never to return. Of course, this raises an immediate question: If this is the largest group, and they don't come back, how come the bars haven't closed down? The answer lies in a simple escalator effect: additional people enter the singles category every day through divorce, the end of a long-term relationship, or other circumstances; for each group of one-timers that pass through and out of the bars, there is a new group ready to take their place.

The second category we noted includes the occasional

bar-goers, people who say they do not particularly like going to bars, but return, without false expectations, when they are bored or lonely. Also included in this group are those who use the bars for a limited time, for a specific purpose, such as the newly uncoupled, who need to reaffirm their attractiveness.

Lastly, there does appear to be a very small group of people who frequent the bars on a regular basis. Whether they belong to the peacock type described by one respondent or are simply lonely, these singles go to the bars on a routine basis. Partly because of this familiarity, for them the singles bar does not appear to have the same elements of a social test, dashed hopes, or threat to self-esteem as it does for other singles.

As researchers, we were intrigued by the attitudes and behaviors reported in our interviews on the singles bars. But we wanted to know whether these observations were really accurate or simply due to the unique circumstances of those interviewed. The most direct way to find out was to see for ourselves. We decided to conduct our own limited field experiment, by going to several singles bars and observing the interactions there.

Being There—A Firsthand View of Singles Bars

We selected two well-known singles bars in a major metropolitan area, one catering to a younger, yuppie crowd, the other to older singles, mostly over forty and divorced.

We chose Friday as the best night for our observations since that was when we expected to find the greatest amount of singles activity. We planned to visit each bar twice to verify that our first impressions were not atypical.

As sociologists, we had both been trained in participation observation, a methodology similar to that used by anthropologists in studying unfamiliar cultures. In its simplest form, participation observation involves becoming immersed in a setting and making systematic observations of the organization, activities, and rituals, to better understand them.

Taylor's (not its real name), the yuppie bar we had chosen for our initial observation, is centrally located on a downtown street corner. Through the huge glass windows, the interior is visible to all who pass by. From the street we could see the oval bar, the small side tables, the polished wooden floors, the ferns in hanging pots, and plenty of fashionably dressed men and women standing, sitting, talking, laughing.

Once inside, the picture was less appealing. The first thing we noticed was the noise level, which tends to grow in decibels as the evening progresses. The noise is caused not only by conversation but by blaring music, and in this case a large-screen TV suspended from the ceiling. Since the noise discourages individual conversation, a major avenue for getting to know someone is immediately closed.

We remarked to the bartender about the loudness of the music, and asked, "How do you expect anyone to talk? They can't hear each other!" He answered, "Are you kidding? If they could hear each other they wouldn't come in here in the first place. This way they don't *have* to talk."

By the time we arrived, at 9:30 P.M., things were just getting under way. All the seats at the bar and tables were taken, but there was still standing room available. An hour later, most of the standing room was gone.

As we watched people arriving, we noticed that none of the women we saw came into the bar alone. They arrived in groups of two or three, a few in groups of four or five. The situation was different for males, who only occasionally arrived in groups. Generally they were in pairs, and unlike the women, many of them came alone. The majority of both men and women appeared to be between twenty-five and thirty-five years old.

We were especially interested in behavior patterns, since so many of those who commented on the bar scene had emphasized an awareness of changed behavior in that setting. They were right. Throughout the evening we observed that, overall, men and women in the bar tended to behave in extremes that fit traditional, stereotypical sex roles (the strong, silent male and the sweet, smiling female waiting to be chosen by him).

Women who in other settings might initiate conversation did not do so here; instead they engaged in what might be called "active passivity." They attempted to look constantly animated, frequently exaggerating their movements with dramatic gestures. They smiled all the time, as though they were saying, "See, I am so much fun to be with." Occasionally they would cast a surreptitious glance around to see if they were being noticed. We could see why people had used adjectives like *fake* and *plastic* to describe the bars. There is something subtle about an artificial smile that gives it less chance of "passing" than a counterfeit bill. The many, many plastered-on smiles had a dampening effect on the general atmosphere. They also created a feeling of sameness, rather than individuality, about the women.

The men in the bar tended to look nonchalant, and disinterested, except when they were approaching a woman. Then they were sometimes gruff and generally more aggressive than in ordinary settings. Normal good manners appeared to be suspended in the bar atmosphere.

An implied sexuality underlies the bar scene, which not only contributes to stereotypical behavior but permits males to take liberties they would not take in another setting. They appear to see women as entering their turf and, as such, subject to their rules—a milder version of "she got what she asked for, didn't she?" A number of men told us that women entering bars must expect certain advances or they wouldn't be there in the first place.

There is no equivalent factor for males in bars, since they have always frequented them. But this does not mean that men are any more comfortable than women in singles bars.

Their advances in this setting often appear to be a hopeful, but clumsy, way to establish contact. The problem is, they are uncertain about the type of contact they want to establish and/or a better way of doing it. As a result, men in singles bars tend to drink more heavily than usual to achieve a measure of relaxation in a situation they find very tension producing. This combination of tension and excessive drinking contributes to the unpleasant behavior often reported in singles bars.

Women, on the other hand, are intimidated enough in bars that they do not exercise their customary prerogative of spelling out the rules by which men must abide. In other settings, a woman's skill at promoting social interaction helps define what is acceptable behavior and what is not. But in this setting, where her actions might be interpreted as aggressive, and somehow compromising, she assumes a more passive role. The result is maximum discomfort and uncertainty.

The patterns we observed at Taylor's were repeated at The Hideaway (again, not the real name), a suburban singles bar for the over-forty crowd. The Hideaway is located near a freeway close to a number of upper-middle-class suburban communities. The parking lot outside was packed with Lincolns, Oldsmobiles, and Cadillacs. We stepped inside to a dark, reddish interior, and a wall of cigarette smoke. A band was playing fifties music, and the tiny dance floor was crowded. Beyond the dance floor there was a scattering of tables, and several steps led up to a mezzanine of mini-bars, where people leaned over drinks to flirt or watch those dancing below.

The clientele was obviously older, mostly in their forties and fifties, with a few over sixty. It was apparent from the type of music and from the number of smokers that these people had grown up in a different period than their younger counterparts. Yet the behavior was very similar to that which we had seen at Taylor's: The women, sitting in small groups, were smiling and trying to look animated; the men were mostly watching, like buyers at an auction, and occasionally asking them to dance. We noticed a greater emphasis on dancing here than at Taylor's. We also noticed the atmosphere was much more depressing: The women appeared more desperate, some wearing clothes that were too tight, and gyrating suggestively on the dance floor. The men, who were also older, were drinking more heavily here and were more outspoken in making somewhat vulgar comments to the women.

We noticed a greater acceptance of touching and general physical contact in this setting. For example, a blonde sitting at the bar allowed herself to be fondled around the shoulders by each man who came to that section of the bar to order a drink. It was apparent she did not know these men, but she appeared to enjoy the contact. When she left that spot, another woman immediately took her place and the last man who had been nuzzling the blonde began to nuzzle the newcomer, who also seemed to enjoy it. This type of bar behavior, characterized by "give me a body, any body," is demoralizing for both men and women because it negates a basic value we have been taught since childhood: "Beauty is only skin deep," or "It's what's inside that counts." The bar scene says, "Who cares what's inside? If you're of the opposite sex and presentable, you'll do."

In both bars we observed that the noise intensified as the evening wore on and more drinks were consumed. Along with the noise and drinking, there was an increase in the density of the crowd, and much more body contact as people moved from one part of the room to another, and found excuses to brush up against each other. Near closing time, it was impossible to move at all without feeling a press of bodies.

Having completed our observations of the bars, we concluded that our interview information had been essentially correct. We also concluded there are two major factors affecting behavior in singles bars: The first is the knowledge that you most likely will never see those people again, which provides a certain anonymity. The second is the perception that in the singles bar no one is interested in you as an individual. This means the personal control (action/reaction) we exert in most social situations is absent from the bar scene.

The result is that the reputation of the singles bar as a one-night stand, whether sexual or social, has become a self-fulfilling prophecy. Why invest your time in the mental and emotional strain of getting to know someone when there will be nothing to show for your effort the next morning?

However, we may now be on the threshold of change. Certainly there have been some alterations in sexual expectations in the singles bars since we first began our interviews three years ago. At that time, the images of the bars and easy sex went hand in hand. As one owner put it, "The bars used to epitomize that old expression, 'Slam, bam, thank you ma'am.' Now no one exactly asks for a medical report, but they do want to know you first. The question, 'Does she or doesn't she'—have the big *A*—gets pretty sinister. Sex is great, but I don't know many people willing to die for it."

Although the level of casual sex associated with singles bars has almost certainly declined, no one really knows how much of it was myth and how much was reality in the first place. But it is doubtful that changes in sexual behavior will transform singles bars into comfortable meeting places, unless they are also accompanied by changes in *social* behavior. The bars are no closer to becoming legitimate meeting places for singles simply because bed-hopping has declined. In addition, they must shed the old stereotypical images and provide an environment that encourages social interaction. Removing the pressure of instant sex from the array of expectations may be the first step in a process that will, over time, transform singles bars in the same way the personals were ultimately transformed, into legitimate vehicles for single men and women to meet.

Mix, Match, and Party Places

For singles seeking a night out, the list of things to do and places to go is seemingly endless: singles dances, singles discussion groups, singles parties, singles sports, and a host of others. Some are geared primarily toward meeting and social activities, while others involve a mutual interest. Discussion groups may include the topic of relationships, but they may also center on things like investment, taxes, home ownership, and other concerns of singles. One of the oldest singles groups, Parents Without Partners, originally intended as a support group for solo parents, has proven for many to be an excellent meeting place.

Although churches no longer function as the natural meeting places they once were, nonetheless a number of denominations have attempted to address the needs of growing numbers of singles by providing space for groups to meet. Many cities advertise groups that are specifically for "separated or divorced Catholics," "Jewish singles," or that function under the umbrella of a specific church. One of the largest singles groups in the Midwest meets at the Unitarian church located in a fashionable suburb. It sponsors a variety of singles programs, including discussion groups, self-improvement activities, and dances.

On asking singles about their experiences with various activities it became clear to us that "stepping out" covers a variety of not only *places*, but of *comfort levels* as well. Singles feel more at ease at a self-improvement seminar for singles than at a singles bar. Other singles places vary in comfort levels, in direct proportion to the stated intent of the event. A travel club for singles is less threatening than a singles dance; folk dancing for singles tends to be more relaxing than cheek-to-cheek singles parties.

The key to the comfort level lies in a certain ambiguity in the stated purpose. It is difficult to pretend at a singles dance that you are not looking. But at a meeting of Parents Without Partners no one really knows if you are present because of little Susie or Sam or mostly to meet someone; perhaps neither do you. This ambiguity has a twofold benefit: First, you are more free to be yourself, which means you will show to your own best advantage, and second, you do not need to protect your self-esteem from feelings of rejection.

Singles told us over and over that issues of need and rejection are some of the most difficult for them to handle. Whenever they enter a new situation, they think about what sort of risk is involved in being too open with their feelings. A thirty-four-year-old woman told us, "You scare people away if they think you're desperate; there's too large an investment."

A forty-two-year-old man said, "The more frustrated you become the more you think in terms of being a loser and present yourself as a loser."

A woman describing her first singles dance told us, "I left after half an hour—I felt like a wallflower at the senior prom."

A twenty-nine-year-old geologist summed it up, "The more you concentrate on finding someone in a social situation, the more people back off. When your need is so strong, you convey it."

One very successful entrepreneur has built his business on low-risk meetings for singles. For several years he has sponsored theme parties at fashionable spots around town. Recent parties have been "Around the World in 80 Days," "New Year's Eve Masked Ball," and a "M*A*S*H Party"; guests are urged to dress for the theme. The parties provide music, dancing, and a cash bar; but the major attraction is activities that are designed to promote nonthreatening interaction, for example, the capturing of "prisoners" at the North/South rebel party. Parties emphasize the concepts of fun and play; the success of these techniques is noted in a party newsletter, which has recently begun to publish notices of wedding bells for couples who have reported meeting at the parties.

Stepping Out, Without Getting Stepped On: Rules for Success

Despite the obstacles, singles continue to experiment with ways of meeting. Trying to find someone on your own is not a bad idea; after all, who knows better than you the sort of person most suited to your tastes and the places you might find him/her? But before you set out to investigate the array of singles meeting places, here are a few suggestions based on our research.

Goal-setting Ask yourself what you want to get out of the evening. Your secret dream might be a glass slipper or a sleeping princess, but tuck that away for now, and think carefully about what will make this a *successful* evening out for you.

Make a list. It may include people-watching, conversation with someone new, physical exercise, getting information, learning something new, or simply getting out of your house or apartment. If you look at the list of singles activities around town, you will probably find several that will match your expectations.

Underlying your list is most likely the goal of *maybe* meeting someone special. The key word is *maybe*. If meeting someone is your only top priority, the evening will be a failure unless you do, and worse yet, you'll feel like one. If, on the other hand, you set a list of reasonable goals before you ever step out the door, chances are you will accomplish enough of them to proclaim the evening a success, and to feel good about it. Anything else, e.g., prince or princess charming falling into your arms on the stroke of midnight, will be an added bonus.

The rehearsal Once you pick the activity that is best suited to your goals, think about how comfortable you will be in the situation you've chosen. A popular treatment for phobias used to begin with having the patient imagine the situation as realistically as possible, including all the feelings that went with it—not a bad technique for singles. Think about yourself and how you would feel, in detail, in the setting you wish to enter. There may be a singles bar that has exactly the music you like, but you recall the only time you went into a bar in the past, you broke out in hives and a cold sweat. Our advice is to pass on that one. If you plunge headfirst into a situation without paying attention to your own feelings, the likelihood is you will feel somewhat out of control, victimized by those same feelings. Remember, an adventuresome setting is not going to suddenly change your normal fears and reactions. If you have always been self-conscious entering a roomful of strangers, you are not going to find it any easier now that you've put your sex appeal on the line as well.

Be practical We have seen singles frequently fall into the same trap of which they accuse their "fixer-upper" friends—assuming all singles are the same. Simply seeking out groups of singles is not enough. Even singles bars vary according to type of neighborhood and social status of clientele. The key factor in finding eligible dating partners is to look for places that *maximize* commonalities. It's unlikely (though not impossible) that you'll find an art lover in a bowling alley, or vice versa.

Go where the fun is... for you If you can't find a place where you think you will have a good time, stay home. It's true, we have all heard the story of someone who didn't want to go out one particular night, was persuaded to go with a friend, and met Mr./Ms. right that very time. It's possible—and if you find yourself saying no to everything, it's probably time to reassess. But, in general, others see you at your best when you are having fun, when you are most animated, enthusiastic, and least self-conscious. It is to your advantage to pick your favorite things to do, not only because you will have the best time, but because they are also the settings that bring out the best in you.

7

Private Strategies

You may be one of those people who would never set foot inside a singles bar, never join a health club if it had any kind of reputation as a singles hangout, and never have anything to do with the personal ads. But neither would you sit at home waiting for the phone to ring or for the right person to knock at the door. So what's left? Plenty!

Over and over, men and women told us why they shy away from the established public strategies and how they have devised their own methods in which the real goal of finding someone is completely hidden. They explained why it feels different to meet someone in one type of situation versus another and why you may sometimes feel like you're suffering from singles burnout—especially if you are female.

Falling somewhere between the covert private strategies and the more flagrant goals of the public meeting methods, some new alternative ways to bring single people together in less intimidating, more relaxed environments have evolved. Take a large single population and complaints about how hard it is to meet one another—and the entrepreneurial juices really begin to flow.

Public vs. Private—The Horror of Letting It All Hang Out

On Thursday nights, David, a thirty-two-year-old real estate lawyer, has a ritual of reading the personal ads in *The Reader*, a weekly "what's happening" paper for the Minneapolis/St. Paul area. He reads through all the ads, even those placed by other men. Despite his curiosity and admitted interest in some of the SWFs each week, David said he could never bring himself to answer an ad or even place one himself: "I think it's great for people who can do it, but I just can't. I know this sounds obnoxious and egotistical, but I still think that the other people doing it may be more desperate than I am, and those aren't the kind of people I want to meet." We heard a similar theme from lots of other people who loved to read the ads but basically told us that it wasn't their style.

Singles bars or dances fall into another category of activity that makes some people shudder. For many of those we spoke with, the common denominator of using personal ads and going to singles functions is the notion that you are going public, not only with your single status, but with your desire to meet someone. In other words you are revealing a piece of personal information about yourself to strangers that you would rather not disclose. Sandy, a thirty-three-year-old Ph.D. student in English, told us, "It would be easier for me to tell someone what color underwear I like to wear than to admit that I am single and looking to meet someone. To do that would make me feel vulnerable."

Sandy believes that a person should be able to find his or her mate in a private way, through everyday happenstance —no advertising in papers or in bars. To do the latter is tantamount to admitting personal failure at a developmental task that she feels most human beings should be able to accomplish without going public.

Consider these two interactions:

1. You are in the checkout line at your local supermarket. As usual you have masterfully picked the worst line. The cashier is unbearably slow and the customer in front of you wrote out a check that had not received prior approval. It looks like you're going to be on line long enough for your ice cream to melt. You shake your head and turn around just

in time to share a sigh of disgust with a nice-looking man who is in line behind you. Your respective grimaces turn into smiles and you begin to talk.

2.   You have placed an ad in the personals column and have decided to meet one of the men who responded and with whom you spoke on the phone. He had a great voice, seemed considerate, and was even able to make some clever comebacks to your not-so-wonderful puns. He suggested meeting for coffee and dessert at a small café that you've been to many times. You are sitting at a table in the corner convinced that Quasimodo with a great personality will be heading for your table. Then another thought, perhaps even worse, enters your mind. Maybe you'll detect some slight look of disappointment on *his* face when he sees *you*. The door opens and there he is—there's no mistaking that searching glance—the look of trying to find someone based purely upon verbal description. Your eyes meet in mutual acknowledgment, you smile politely, and he joins you at your table.

If we analyze these two situations we can see why Sandy and many others feel the way they do about personal ads and other such strategies for meeting one another. In the first scenario, the two people will talk and if all goes well, one or the other will try and lead the conversation in the direction of a future meeting. Assuming there are no clues to their marital or parenthood status, such as a wedding ring or boxes of Pampers sticking out of the shopping cart, the person who initiates the idea of a date, which is still most likely the man, has to put himself on the line. But the interaction can be handled in a number of ways because there was no "intent" to the meeting in the first place—just two people doing their shopping. Even if the main reason they shop at that particular store is to meet someone, nobody knows that but themselves. The interaction can be managed in a way that makes it secondary to their apparent purpose, which is to buy groceries.

People who have used these more "natural" strategies find they have to work harder at uncovering the basic facts—such as the other person's marital status, availability, and interest in dating. However, there is greater freedom in the interaction because each person's singleness and desire to meet someone is privately held information. Depending upon the feelings of both people, that information may or may not be shared. You may get into a discussion about hot peppers and decide to meet someplace for Mexican food. As you discover more about your feelings for one another, whatever they may be, the interaction can adjust accordingly. But at least from the start, all options are available: friendly acquaintance, not-so-friendly acquaintance, good friends, or lovers, to name a few.

In the second scenario, the intent is clear. The situation has been defined: Two single people are looking to meet someone. Regardless of the fact that personal ads have gained considerable acceptability as a medium for bringing people together, by writing or responding to an ad you are implicitly agreeing to participate in a situation that involves joint expectations about appearances, personalities, and the short- and long-term outcomes of the meeting. Furthermore, joint expectations often involve rejection and disappointment.

By using personal ads you relinquish some control over the dynamics of the interaction. Some people, like Sandy, tell us the intent of the meeting is too focused and revealing. Your availability and interest in dating is no longer an issue to be discovered—it is a known fact. Sometimes even your interest in the person you meet must be decided in a relatively short time because the whole purpose of the meeting is to find a lasting, long-term, and romantic relationship. It is as though you must assess the potential for that type of relationship over a few cups of coffee and some cheesecake.

Formal participation in defined singles activities creates the stress of specific expectations—the most obvious of which is finding a mate. To have made the formal effort with nothing to show for it can often make people feel worse than they did before they even started.

See You at the Veggies

In order to avoid the public declaration, people have developed private strategies for transforming everyday activities and places into potential meeting places. Like trained observers, they have taken mental notes of the organization of life around them. Some commuters to New York City know which are the better trains to catch and which are the better cars to sit in. As one of these commuters, Cheryl told us, "If you're going to be on the train three hours a day, fifty weeks a year, you might as well make the most of it and try and help your social life at the same time." Cheryl works mostly with other women in a nonprofit research organization and feels that her only real chances of meeting a man occur while she is commuting to work or on weekends.

Private strategies make perfect sense. It's not cold and calculating to consider where and when you may have the best chances of meeting the kind of person you think you would be interested in. Would you look for a Colnago racing bike in your local family bicycle store, or a Monet print at K-Mart? Of course not. Why should the logic and common sense that pervades the rest of your life go by the wayside simply because finding someone with whom to have a meaningful relationship is categorized as a matter of the heart—something to be left up to fate?

Rhonda, a twenty-six-year-old window designer, recently accepted a new job in Manhattan but settled in a northern suburban community. She told us that in order to expose herself to more young unmarried people, male or female, she got out the yellow pages and listed the supermarkets and laundromats in all the surrounding towns. She made a point of going to different ones at different times so that she could get a feel for the clientele. On Sundays, she rode around on her bicycle to check out various places to buy the Sunday paper, as well as to identify popular jogging routes. Since Rhonda was actually a serious runner, she searched for the more challenging hills and scenic routes and found out about regional races through the local athletic clothing store. Is Rhonda obsessed, unhealthy, or desperate because she drives two extra miles to buy her milk at Finast instead of Safeway, or is she simply maximizing her potential to meet someone she might be interested in?

Alexa, a thirty-eight-year-old focus group moderator who is an avid reader, goes to the New York Public Library reading rooms rather than her living room to enjoy her favorite hobby: "I look for a table with some interesting people at it and see what happens. At least I'm out there rather than holed up in my own apartment."

For the athletically inclined, pursuing a favorite sport is the most natural way to meet people. Running, roller skating, cross-country and downhill skiing were often mentioned as private strategies for meeting someone, particularly because you can participate in them without being dependent on anyone else. Becky, a twenty-seven-year-old court reporter, loves to play tennis. On weekends, before the courts are crowded, she grabs a bucketful of balls and practices her serves. If she is lucky, another solo tennis player will come by looking for a partner. She accepts—whether male or female. Otherwise, if she is forced off the court by a twosome, she heads for the backboards and practices her strokes. "I've got nothing to lose," Becky told us, "I love to play the game. The way I look at it, if I don't meet some great guy that I think I can fall in love with, I'm still developing a great tennis game. You just never know: You play tennis with someone and then eventually you get invited to a party and meet other people. I just believe that if you give off good vibes you get them back."

Art festivals, street fairs, flea markets, and antiques shows are popular havens for singles. First of all, unlike some other nonparticipatory events (such as concerts or listening to music at a bar), most people are comfortable going to them on their own. They are fun, unstructured, filled with people, and provide lots of opportunities to meet others.

Although private strategies differ from more formal efforts to meet someone, such as the personal ads, they too come equipped with their disappointments. Private strategies, by definition, are typically embedded in everyday activities and personal interests—but something else has been added to them. Yes, the laundry or shopping still gets done, and the five-mile jog still gets run, but attached to each activity is the thought and the hope that you will experience the bonus of meeting someone special. When that doesn't happen there is a twinge of disappointment—but at least no one else knows about it.

Truth and Consequences

Private strategies are used to some extent by almost all singles, albeit with varying levels of seriousness and conscious intent. Recently, a number of women's magazines have attempted to provide women with private strategies for meeting men. Perhaps the most insulting messages that some magazines and books give to singles are recipes for meeting a man or woman that leave the uniqueness of *you* out of the ingredients. One recent article recommended that women research the location of a convention of lawyers, travel to the site, and relax in the lobby or coffee shop, in a nicely appointed business suit. Another suggestion was to join a local political campaign, which was likely to be dominated by intelligent, ambitious men. One woman who read the article said the first suggestion seemed "downright deceptive and cheap," but few people would find the second suggestion objectionable if you really have an interest in local politics and the candidate for whom you volunteer.

But let's be honest: It just doesn't make sense to join a runners club if the thought of a walk around the block makes you breathless, or a mountain-climbing club if you are scared of heights. Even if you are lucky enough to meet someone interesting, you will have begun a new friendship on a note of deception.

All of us attribute characteristics to people we don't know based upon what we can observe, such as looks, clothing, height, weight, voice, behavior, where they live, or the car they drive. Group affiliations are also important indicators of who we are, what is important to us, our values, and our life-style. For example, if you saw a car with NATIONAL RIFLE ASSOCIATION and VOTE FOR BUSH bumper stickers you would probably be safe in assuming the person had a fairly conservative bent. Since people are generally consistent in the nature of their views from one situation to the next, you could probably conjure up accurate predictions of the person's stand on a number of other social and political issues. On the other hand, if someone drove by in a car plastered with bumper stickers such as I BRAKE FOR ANIMALS, SAVE THE WHALES, or VEGETARIAN SOCIETY OF AMERICA, you would make drastically different assumptions.

Everyone uses information such as group affiliations and appearance to draw conclusions about people they don't know. If you join a running club, you would expect to find people who share your passion for running, take care of their bodies, watch their diets, and do not smoke. Joining groups for the sole purpose of meeting someone, without sincerely sharing in the fundamental purpose of the club is dishonest to both yourself and others. You are not just looking to meet any man or any woman but you are looking to meet someone to whom you can relate, with whom you share some common values and beliefs.

Airing Your Dirty Laundry

He walks into the laundromat and asks for starched collars and a glass of white wine. She is at the supermarket on a

Wednesday night about to reach for the Philadelphia Cream Cheese when she is asked to dance. What's happening? Private strategies are going public.

Media attention to the aging baby boomers, delayed marriage, and increased divorce have put the consumer spotlight on the needs, wants, and life-styles of single people. Frozen food companies were quick to package gourmet meals in individual servings, astute real estate developers put their dollars into condos and co-ops with the message of "maintenance-free living," and organizations such as the National Association of Single Persons were set up to provide financial and tax counseling tailored to the special needs of single people. Once these more pragmatic needs were taken care of, creative entrepreneurs and even relatively staid organizations began to recognize a burgeoning market for alternative meeting places for singles.

There's nothing like a bottle of Clorox and a basket of dirty laundry for reducing the intimidation factor. In some cities, the answer to the singles bar is a laundromat, bar, and deli all in one. Customers load the washers and dryers and then slip across to the other side of the glass partition where they can sip wine and munch on appetizers and sandwiches. Not only is it a painless way to get your laundry done but people are relaxed—and more open to meeting one another.

On most days, aisle number four at a Boston supermarket holds canned fruits and vegetables and bottled water. On this particular Saturday, it held a wedding party. The bride and groom in traditional wedding attire stood at the spot where they met nine months earlier, surrounded by family and friends. It had not been simply a happenstance meeting over the Evian and Perrier but the result of singles night at a nearby supermarket. While some owners have simply transplanted the trappings of the singles bar to their produce section, others have tried to be more creative by providing ice-breaking games, name tags, aerobic workouts, and lots of free samples. The motivation is not the altruistic desire of supermarket owners to help the plight of singles trying to meet one another but rather the fact that singles contribute to a substantial proportion of the stores' daily receipts.

Are you concerned about the intertidal shallows off the Maine coast? Interested in the underwater environment of a coral reef? If you are, you should have attended the "eco-mixer" sponsored by the venerable Smithsonian Institution at the National Museum of Natural History. Between lectures and discussion groups, time was set aside for mingling, munching, and sipping wine. Similar singles events were held at the National Museum of American Art, the National Air and Space Museum, and the Baltimore Museum of Art. The appeal of these events, apart from the chance to learn about our planet's ecology or that of Pluto, is the belief that more educated, wholesome, non–singles bar people will attend these functions. Of course, museum administrators stand to gain too, since their overriding concern is increasing public participation in their programs.

Church as meeting place is trying to make a comeback. The Unitarian Universalist Society in a northern Westchester suburb recently offered weekly Friday evening gatherings to discuss topics such as "How Singles Manage Money," "What Have You Discovered About Yourself in the Last Year?" (choice of discussion or dance), "How to Be Creative in Forming Friendships," and "The Frightening Four-Letter Word." Wine, cheese, talk, and mingling are yours for four dollars a session.

The Sutton Place Synagogue on Manhattan's fashionable East Side has tried to bring Jewish singles together for the High Holy Days, since many of them no longer have family or relatives in the area with whom they can share the holidays. To accommodate the great demand, Rosh Hashanah services have been held at the Waldorf Astoria. After services, people have a chance to meet one another as they share in a holiday feast.

There is an air of familiarity to each of these examples. Why? Because each of these alternative attempts at attracting singles has evolved from already existing private strategies of millions of singles. It is almost accepted folklore if not common knowledge that laundromats and supermarkets hold the potential for meeting someone interesting of the opposite sex, and "cruising" in a car creates images dating back to the 1930s. A stroll through the museum on a lazy Sunday afternoon not only guarantees Renoir, but has always held the potential for a captivating meeting with an attractive and cultured stranger. It's the stuff that movies are made of! Finally, we provide evidence of some effort on the part of church or synagogue to reclaim its role as a meeting place for single men and women.

Private Strategies Go Public— A Double-Edged Sword

Single men and women need new institutions and new rules for finding one another. The formalization of private strategies as described above has provided some alternatives. However, only time will tell whether these new forms will take on the undesirable characteristics of singles bars or whether they will retain their current unique status.

The double-edged sword of these new developments is that while they provide a more relaxed, natural environment in which to meet, they also bring the issue of intent closer to the forefront. Going to a laundromat that many young single people tend to patronize and hoping that you may happen to meet someone interesting is different from going to a laundromat that has been set up with the rather explicit dual purpose of doing your laundry and meeting someone of the opposite sex—and not necessarily in that order. Along with the validation of an activity or place as a "singles meeting place" come rules and expectations. Would you feel comfortable going to a bar-laundromat dressed in laundry day clothes—the ones that we all keep in the bottom of our drawer to be worn only when everything else is already in the laundry basket? Can you just run to the supermarket to pick up a quart of milk, knowing it's singles night? Or will the normative behaviors and manner of dressing at such laundromats and grocery stores become stilted and unrelaxed?

The way in which a situation is perceived, what sociologists call the "definition of the situation," has a direct impact on subsequent interactions and behaviors. If a health club gains the reputation of being a singles hot spot, you can still do your workout, but it is no longer just a gym. The bar-laundromat is not just a laundromat nor is the Pathmark just a supermarket on Wednesday nights. If a local café that you routinely frequented on Sunday mornings suddenly started advertising itself as a great place for singles to meet, you would probably start looking for a new hangout. It would have lost its appeal. When your single marital status is the public drawing card, the rules for interaction change.

The Energy Factor—Showing Your Peacock Feathers

Whether you go the public route or the private one, there is one common underlying element: You are making an effort to meet someone—and effort means energy. Joan, a thirty-seven-year-old recruiter for an executive placement service, told us she was thirteen months into a serious relationship with Chris, a man she had met on her way to a concert they were both attending. She recounted the disappointments of earlier relationships and her changing expectations as she evolved from each one—but most of all Joan talked about "energy." The most drastic change that she had noticed since her involvement with Chris was the feeling of relief that came from *not* expending energy on her personal life. Of course, in reality this was not exactly true, but Joan had never before realized how much mental and physical energy she had spent as a single person seriously interested

ific physical energy is more restricted to those activi-
behaviors in which you choose to engage such as
ng, dressing, or preparing for an evening on the
Although these are activities that are practiced by
e, not just singles, singles are more likely to focus on
nce-related behaviors than those who are not inter-
meeting someone of the opposite sex.

did Joan focus so much on the idea of "energy"
e interviewed her? Let's face it, for someone in a
relationship or who is married, doing the laundry, or
g for food or clothes is simply that. There is no hid-
nda or need for special primping other than what
uld ordinarily do. This is not to imply that a Dr.
Mr. Hyde transformation accompanies an "I do,"
to suggest that when you are not interested in meet-
eone of the opposite sex, there is less relative energy
d on appearance and less awareness of or response
ous signals from the men or women around you.

omen Look and Men Don't

point you are probably asking yourself why we
written about the private strategies of men. The ap-
as in this chapter also bothered us, to the point that
mined the data from our focus groups and personal
s. What we came up with was the unsettling con-
at private strategies appear to be more characteris-
men's behavior than men's. Now, to two female
ts, one of whom came of age during the women's
t, some explanation was necessary.

ample reference in the literature on gender differ-
upport the fact that woman, not man, is the more
nal. Carol Gilligan, in her book entitled *A Differ-*
demonstrates how men and women have different
ns to the world around them. Women focus on at-
and social relationships, men on autonomy. Some

---

in finding a mate: "I became the World Book Encyclopedia
of things to do and places to go. Basically, I was never home,
and if I was I couldn't enjoy it because I might be missing
out on something or someone really good."

Have you ever gone to a party that you really didn't want
to go to? You smile a lot and mingle like you're supposed to,
but as soon as you get into your car and close the door, you
feel absolutely drained. Or how about a first date that just
isn't working out. You try to accept the evening for what it
is and at least share some good food with your companion.
But the evening drags on—the service has never been
slower—and afterward you have to wait an eternity for a
cab. It has only been two and a half hours since you left
your apartment, but when you return home you feel like
you've put in an eight-hour day at the office.

Although any relationship requires time and energy, the
search for a meaningful one is the ultimate energy sapper.
Assuming you are interested in settling down with someone,
can you think of any other task that permeates so many
aspects of your life and so many hours of every day? Like
Joan, you may not even be aware of how much energy you
are putting out until you are no longer required to do so.

Energy takes on different forms. First, there is mental energy, which can be broken down into two categories, generalized and specific. Generalized mental energy is that which
is spent, often in a subconscious way, hoping that you will
finally meet the kind of person in whom you could be interested. If you had your mind set on an important job promotion within a certain number of years, you would be
concerned with your performance on any minor or major
task along the way. Similarly with your personal life. For
those who are interested in settling down with someone, it's
like a major developmental task—a promotion. In other
words, your desires and hopes are not simply abstract motivations that you activate on occasion, but are emotional
drives that are the backdrop to many of your everyday

thoughts and activities. This kind of energy is probably the most difficult to measure since it is part and parcel of your being until its function has been served.

Specific mental energy is more focused and deliberate. It is the kind of energy that you might spend trying to optimize your chances of meeting someone through your ordinary everyday activities, such as shopping or doing the laundry—what we refer to as private strategies. Janet, a thirty-nine-year-old travel agent, confided that she is not very spontaneous anymore about when and where she carries out her errands. In describing her weekly trip to the local Path-mark, Janet told us, "It's not that I completely change what I'm going to do on any given day, but I do make slight alterations. For example, I'm an early riser—even on weekends. Part of me would like to get my grocery shopping done at eight in the morning—I don't have to hassle with all the people and then I have the rest of the day to do more fun things. But I decided I won't go—because I feel that I have to try and be around more people if I'm ever going to meet someone, and an empty grocery store is not the answer."

While it may not compare to a workout on the Nautilus equipment, involvement in the search for a mate also requires considerable physical energy, which like mental energy, can be broken down into the general and the specific. General physical energy is what many singles described to us as the feeling of being "on." Like other species of animals, humans display ritualized behaviors when involved in courtship and flirtation. When a woman or man enters a crowded singles bar, noticeable changes occur: slight alterations in posture, increased facial expressions, hair primping, eye movements, changes that are registered by your body and ultimately expend energy. These kinds of adjustments are constantly being made whenever the situation becomes defined as one in which you want to attract someone's attention or respond in a flirtatious manner.

When we observed interactions at singles bars, flirtatious

behaviors between men and wo
picture. In singles bars, even the
of the same sex are energy lade
hidden dimensions to the intera
expectations for appropriate beh
refer to as role playing. It was
formation in people—women,
tered the bars. It was almost as
some incredibly funny joke as
old. Groups of two or three wo
bar and almost immediately
complete with facial and gestur

There is really nothing myst
behaviors. They merely reflec
men are more attracted to wor
and do not appear weighed do
to say that women friends do
when they go out together,
singles bar one is participatir
appropriate behavior. Perhap
the artificiality of singles ba
only a small slice of a person
posed—that part which is
less, the generalized energ
substantial. As Tina, a tw
put it, "It's like all of my sen
engaged in a conversation,
aware of everyone in my lin
aware of me, taking walks
opportune times if I particu
By the end of the evenin
physical energy occurs alm
fine the situation as one in
traction. This could occur
or environment such as w
sitting in a restaurant.

theorists claim that the difference between men and women evolves from women's socialization into more nurturant roles. One proscriptive element of the female role concerns being vulnerable, tender, emotional, open, and warm. Others attribute the difference to the reproductive ability of women—their unique role in the continuation of the species.

Whatever the reason, the difference between men and women with regard to social ties and the nature of their relationships is something most of us can relate to. Women's friendships tend to be more intense with other women as well as with men. Women tend to keep in touch with their friends if they move far away. Even if they speak on the phone only once or twice a year, there is an instantaneous and deep, personal connection between good female friends. They begin sharing personal information about their lives and relationships within minutes. There is no secret to their priorities. With men, on the other hand, there is often the glaring omission of personal information during a phone conversation between two "close" male friends. Jobs, sports, health, cars—yes. The nature or dynamics of their relationship, or feelings about not having one—no. In *The McGill Report on Male Intimacy* by Michael E. McGill, relationships between men are described as often shallow and superficial. While women derive solace and support from the intimacy of their friendships, men do not.

The fact that women are deeply rooted in their social connections has been linked to their greater mental health and longevity. Research has shown that the happiest man is a married man. In fact, married men are happier than married women. The reason appears to be that women can derive a great deal of intimacy and social support from the social network they build for themselves. They are not as dependent on the marriage as men are for sharing their thoughts and feelings. Often a man's wife is his only friend—and his only source of intimacy.

Similarly, the quality of life of widows generally outshines that of widowers. Why? Consider the typical scenario. Throughout the years of the marriage, the wife creates and maintains the ties with friends and relatives. She buys and sends the Christmas cards, remembers the birthdays and anniversaries, invites people to dinner, and calls or writes to keep in touch with people of special importance. If the husband dies, she can activate her network and begin to fill the void in her life. There may be other pragmatic skills she needs to learn, tasks that her husband usually took care of, but building social skills is not one of them. If the wife dies first, however, the husband suffers, not only from the loss of a loved one but from the reduced ability to bring intimacy into his life through other contacts. He must begin to develop social skills that are often totally alien to him.

While men may appear to be the aggressors in the singles bars or other formal singles functions, current research that has measured flirtatious behaviors (e.g., primping, eye contact, smiling, broad glances around the room) has found women more likely to be the initiators than men. It appears that women give the initial signal to a man that they find him attractive or might like to meet him and the man then approaches the woman.

Based on our interviews, women take on more responsibility for finding a mate. That is, the private strategies and day-to-day consciousness of looking for a mate seems to fall more within the realm of women. This should not bring to mind visions of women ensnaring men but rather the greater skill that women have in developing relationships and their greater conscious recognition of the importance of intimacy in their lives.

8

Nothing Works Like Success

There are always a few people who appear unaffected by trends or even calamities. Whether it's resourcefulness, smarts, or an extra dose of good luck, these are the people who just happen to have a canoe in their backyard when the flood hits or an extra fuse on hand when the circuits overload. They are the sort who tend to view an emergency as a challenge and a near catastrophe as a minor setback. In the world of meeting and dating, these are the singles who call the shots. When they wish to marry, they always seem to find someone. We interviewed these former singles to discover what they thought was the secret of their success.

The Strategists

Monica is thirty-six, attractive, and runs her own consulting firm. Three years ago she decided it was time to get married. She told us, "I never dated much, simply because there wasn't time. Getting a business on its feet and pursuing a career is more than a full-time job. My dates were mostly casual. Someone would call to go out for dinner or a drink —often it was with their clients and they knew I handled myself well in those situations. These guys weren't in any way serious about me, and the feeling was mutual. I needed someone new. When I looked around the familiar places, they didn't seem very promising. So I approached the problem the way I would a marketing issue. Where do you find the right clientele for the product? I was looking for someone who was professional, but at the same time health minded—or at least had some interest in physical fitness. I joined the Sierra Club and decided to go on only the long hikes; guys who went on those would have a real outdoor spirit. Besides, most of the women would opt for the short little jaunts, and I figured I would have the field to myself. I know that sounds pretty strategic, and some women might be embarrassed by that, but I'm not. I'm paid to be strategic. I just applied some of my own expertise to my situation. I hate to say this, because it sounds so pat, but I met my husband on the first hike! You get to know an awful lot about someone trudging ten or fifteen miles with them. And of course we didn't decide to marry after one long stroll in the woods, but it was a solid beginning."

Monica's husband is a thirty-seven-year-old account executive for an advertising firm, and according to Monica, "He didn't have a clue that the Sierra Club was more than just a club for me. Later, when I told him about my 'master plan,' I thought he might be a little annoyed. But he just laughed and said that is one of the things he likes about me, that I know what I want and go for it."

When we asked her if she would recommend that women in general follow her strategy, she was hesitant: "It's not something you can just tell women to do—they have to be comfortable with it."

Other women told us the same thing: "You have to know what you want and what you like, and if there is a place where eligible men with those interests would go. You can't just fake an interest in something; you could wind up with a husband, but find yourself spending the rest of your life faking it."

One woman was reminded of her grandmother's story: "She and her best friend were both twenty-two, and they met a handsome Italian at their church. The friend invited him for dinner and cooked a real Italian dish, laced with onion and garlic. My grandmother hated garlic and knew her friend did too; she also knew that while the friend was cooking up a storm, she didn't have a chance. The friend finally married the handsome Italian, and my grandmother was heartbroken—at first. Her friend confided a few months later that whenever she tried to cook a dish without garlic, her husband was furious. 'I'm doomed,' she told my grandmother. 'That's what I get for lying. Hell must be a garlic kitchen.' "

When you are trying to decide which places are best for meeting that special someone, remember that a lifetime is a long time to pretend. For example, if you think "proof" refers exclusively to an exercise in logic, you may want to pass on the numismatists convention, and if you hate to cook, forget the course in gourmet dining. But if you're genuinely interested in investment, renovating old houses, or learning basic auto maintenance, enroll in a course or join a club; it may provide the introduction to the perfect person for you. If not, it's far from a total loss. You've at least had an opportunity to learn and to spend your time on something you enjoy.

The Joiners

The joiners differ from the strategists primarily by their "generalist" approach. These singles join groups not so much for a specific type of person or to fulfill a particular goal, but simply to get out and meet others. They assume the rest of the equation will take care of itself.

Glenn, a thirty-three-year-old computer engineer, was married six months ago to a woman he met as the result of his joining efforts. "I have always been pretty shy around women," he told us, "and I just decided if I was ever going to get married, it was now or never. The first thing I did was pure cliché. I actually enrolled in an aerobics class after work; the main reason I did it was because I heard it would be mostly women. That part was true; there was only one other guy, and about twenty-five women. But it wasn't quite what it sounds like; half of those women were married, and the other half looked like they were in the class because they really needed it.

"Luckily I didn't stop with the exercise class. About the same time I started working on a political campaign, and joined a discussion group at the Unitarian church. After a few weeks I quit the exercise group and went back to biking, which I really like; but I stayed with the political campaign and discussion group, because they were interesting by themselves. That's how I met Karen. She must have been born with a campaign sticker on her backside—she loves that stuff. I was impressed at how well-informed she is. We started having coffee after putting in our volunteer hours, and pretty soon it became a routine thing that we would see each other a couple of times a week. I couldn't let her get away just because the campaign was over, so I asked her to marry me."

In the course of our interviews we discovered that some of the most interesting clubs are frequently overlooked because they do not have high visibility. Becky, a thirty-three-year-old advertising manager, told us she had been frustrated at the number of men she met who were clearly unsuitable: "I thought about how people used to talk about going to 'socials' of one sort or another. I wasn't sure exactly what that meant. When I was a kid there used to be ice cream socials at our school, and sometimes there would be a church social, but you don't hear about things like that today. At least I didn't think so until I picked up the newspaper one day and read an article about a woman from Poland who had met her husband at the Polish American Club in her town. The picture caught my eye because they were both in Polish costume. It turned out he was American born, and she had come to this country two or three years ago. I thought to myself, 'Wait a minute. This is a woman from another country, and she's here less than two years and finds a nice, eligible, single guy. How did she do it?' She joined a social club—an ethnic social club."

Becky pointed out that she, along with most people, tended to think of ethnic clubs as organizations for immigrants; but these days most of them have turned into organizations to keep alive an awareness of heritage. "I thought it couldn't hurt to join one, so I joined the Irish American club. It really is interesting; a little like a small town in the middle of a big world. The people you meet, single or not, have a lot in common with you from the beginning. I suppose it's because our parents had so much in common—we were raised in similar ways, with similar values. I met my husband there after about six months, but I liked the club and the people so much, I would have stayed active regardless; as a matter of fact I have, both of us have."

For people who like to join groups, the possibilities are endless. One man told us he met his current wife in a cave, during a spelunking club outing: "She dropped her flashlight from a ledge and it landed on my foot. I thought my toe was broken. I had to sit out the rest of the exploration and she came back to keep me company because she figured it was her fault. We had the whole afternoon to get acquainted. It was great."

Marlene, a twenty-eight-year-old army nurse and second lieutenant, told us we had overlooked one basic American institution: "Some girls join the army for the specific purpose of meeting men. I'm not just talking about bimbos; there are plenty of really nice girls who view the army as an adventure where they can experience a totally different lifestyle and meet lots of eligible men at the same time. I met my husband at the officers club. We discovered we were both from Denver, and even knew some of the same people. My tour of duty will be up in a few months, but we didn't want to wait that long. We were married five months ago."

Alex, a thirty-six-year-old attorney, met his wife of three years at a potluck supper. "I know it sounds pretty mundane," he told us, "but I think it's a good argument for keeping up with ordinary activities in ordinary places."

He had been married for five years and divorced for two,

when he decided it was time to start getting back into things. A married friend, a woman, gave him what he still considers a valuable piece of advice: "She told me not to get involved in activities just for singles, but to do some of the community stuff I had done and liked when I was married. She said that way I would meet compatible people, and there wouldn't be the extra singles pressure. It turned out to be the best thing for me. True, I also met a lot of married people, but that was okay. I had a chance to get used to going to things alone—which I would never have done before—and being comfortable in those situations. I turned from the strong, silent type, into Mr. Congenial. But like a lot of guys, it never was 'strong, silent,' it was 'embarrassingly shy,' but no one knew it. Valerie and I belonged to the same potluck supper group. We sat next to each other a few times and she was so much fun to talk to that I invited her over for a small group supper—just for two. That was the real beginning for us; we were married a year later."

Of course there are always people who join groups for reasons that have nothing to do with meeting someone. A Boston couple told us they met because they owned apartments in the same co-op: "Neither of us would have joined anything just to meet someone. We don't have time. Luckily Sam and I were both on the co-op board. We have such hectic schedules; I can't imagine how we ever would have met otherwise."

If none of the clubs or organizations in your area appeal to you or if they simply do not address your needs, you might consider the solution of Julia, a dance therapist, who has always loved the theater. Recently divorced, she had elected to stay in the same house so her two elementary school children would not have to cope with disrupted friendships. But most of her neighbors were "married with family," and not interested in extra activities. Julia decided to start her own group for single theater-goers; they would attend the performances together, then gather at someone's home to discuss what they had seen.

She told us, "I wouldn't exactly say I love him because he loves Strindberg, but it helps. Stuart joined our group after about six months; he also had been recently divorced. The nice thing about the group was that we had the fun of dating without any of the unpleasantness. You didn't have to ask anyone to go out with you, so there wasn't any worry over being turned down. The same thing was true for the 'who pays' issue. It was all very nice. You were able to be with people at social events, without any of the personal responsibility. By the time Stuart asked me out alone, we already knew each other and could really enjoy ourselves. We were married last year. He says he feels very lucky, that he would have never even met me if it hadn't been for the club. That's probably true; he doesn't take any initiative when it comes to meeting people."

The Advertisers

Those who have been out of circulation for a long time told us the only way to start dating again is to do it. Ruth had been widowed when she was only thirty and was left to raise two little boys. She put most of her energy into her work as a geologist and raising her sons.

"I did not date at all during those years," she told us. "I felt it wouldn't be fair to ask the boys to accept a new father, and I would resent another man trying to tell them what to do. Two years ago my second son went off to college, and almost immediately I sat down and wrote an ad for the eligibles column. You wouldn't believe the answers I got—some of them were pretty suggestive. A neighbor of mine asked to see the ad, and then told me it was all wrong. I didn't answer any of that first batch of letters; instead I wrote another ad. This time it was very direct. Basically I said I was looking for a serious relationship that could lead to marriage. I got only five replies. I called three of the guys, and wound up marrying Mitch. It was wonderful."

Not surprisingly, Ruth wholeheartedly recommends the eligibles column as the way to find someone, especially if you have been out of circulation for a while. But advertising by itself is not enough. Ruth also brought two special ingredients to the want-ad scene: determination and a realistic attitude. A lot of singles would have quit after the first ad; they are the ones who throw their hands up in despair when something doesn't work, and say, "See, I knew only creeps answered these ads."

Not only was Ruth willing to learn from her mistakes, but she was also able to be candid in the ad, and with herself: "It helped having a friend as a sounding board. It's hard to say outright that you want to get married—let alone say it in the newspaper for everyone to see. Of course, nobody knows it's you until they call, but it still is hard. It eliminates some of the coquettishness that's sort of fun at first. But it also saves a lot of time and a lot of misunderstanding. Men who use the ads just to broaden their social life would never have answered my second one."

David also found his wife through the personals. "At first I wouldn't have considered one of those things," he recalled. "I thought the people in them were fictitious...too plastic to be real. On the other hand, I knew a couple of guys who had placed ads, and they were just like everyone else. I started to think about it. Most people aren't born writers, and that's what the ads are: a piece of writing to attract someone. Before I placed my ad, I went around for a few days saying to myself, 'What I really want is...' and 'What I really am like is...' I listened to myself, when I was trying to be spontaneous, and that's how I put my ad together. I don't remember the exact words, but I said something about looking for a woman who understood the lure of winter wilderness and could enjoy a whole evening of reading together in the same room. Beth is a very quiet type; she said she always read the ads, but never intended to answer any of them. The 'winter wilderness' caught her eye. She's one of those people who's hooked on winter camping. Anyway, she wrote to me

...I called her...and we hit it off from the first meeting. I had eight other responses, but I didn't even call anyone else. We were married just six months after we met."

In the Neighborhood

Some singles have no objection to using the personals column as a way of meeting, but find the planning involved in writing an ad and the diligence required in the follow-up are just more organizational tasks they do not need.

Pamela, an internal auditor for a major corporation, spends over 30 percent of her time traveling. "I do best in spontaneous situations," she told us. "It's partly because when I'm away so much, I don't like to plan very far ahead. I might get back from a trip and find I don't want to do any of the things I committed myself to before I left."

According to Pamela, neighborhood is the vital ingredient when you are trying to meet someone. Her experience seems to verify this. "I was on my way to the mail box one morning; it was 7:30 A.M. and I was eating a piece of raisin pie for breakfast. As I was juggling the pie and the letter, Joseph came along and opened the mailbox for me. He had these wonderful dark eyes, and he was laughing. I must have looked pretty odd with my briefcase in one hand and my raisin pie in the other. He asked me if I was a nutritionist. We said a few more things. I discovered he lived only a few blocks from my apartment. He asked for my phone number and I gave him my business card. A few days later, he called. That was over a year ago. We were married last month — on the twenty-second. He says he wanted to go out with me because he had to see if anyone who was that congenial at 7:30 in the morning could keep it up all day."

Pamela illustrates the truism "It pays to be nice." Her strategy was different from the others we spoke with because, on the surface, it wasn't a strategy at all. She is one of those people who meets others easily, whether at mailboxes or window shopping, which was how she had met her previous boyfriend.

But Pamela claims she definitely did have a strategy, even though she only used it on the few occasions she moved. Her strategy was taking great care in choosing the area where she would live. The neighborhood where she met her husband (and still lives) has a reputation for being peopled with younger, upwardly mobile singles. It seems designed for people who like to be out and about, with its ice cream parlors, bookstores, specialty shops, and half a dozen ethnic restaurants. Happy hours abound. The atmosphere is festive and conducive to casual conversation.

Pamela told us, "I knew I didn't have time to join things; besides, I don't like belonging to clubs and going to group events. But I've always been very good at meeting people wherever I happened to be. If I lived in a slum, all my friends would be slum friends, because that's who I would talk to. So when I moved here I made sure I found a neighborhood that I liked; I knew that I would like the people in it—although I didn't know at the time I would like them well enough to marry one."

Singles frequently told us both lack of time and an endless variety of people to choose from favor the wisdom of picking your places and activities to ensure that those you do meet will have at least some initial similarity with you. People often choose neighborhoods with a commonality in mind, but then do not take the time to get out and explore much further than the garage.

Amy, a forty-two-year-old divorced history teacher and mother of three, told us she never expected to find her present husband only three blocks down the street: "I thought average city neighborhoods were filled with average families. I keep forgetting how often things like divorce are part of the 'average' family experience. I was just taking my usual evening walk when I met Joel. He was working in the yard, and we exchanged a few words. Then somehow we in finding a mate: "I became the World Book Encyclopedia of things to do and places to go. Basically, I was never home, and if I was I couldn't enjoy it because I might be missing out on something or someone really good."

Have you ever gone to a party that you really didn't want to go to? You smile a lot and mingle like you're supposed to, but as soon as you get into your car and close the door, you feel absolutely drained. Or how about a first date that just isn't working out. You try to accept the evening for what it is and at least share some good food with your companion. But the evening drags on—the service has never been slower—and afterward you have to wait an eternity for a cab. It has only been two and a half hours since you left your apartment, but when you return home you feel like you've put in an eight-hour day at the office.

Although any relationship requires time and energy, the search for a meaningful one is the ultimate energy sapper. Assuming you are interested in settling down with someone, can you think of any other task that permeates so many aspects of your life and so many hours of every day? Like Joan, you may not even be aware of how much energy you are putting out until you are no longer required to do so.

Energy takes on different forms. First, there is mental energy, which can be broken down into two categories, generalized and specific. Generalized mental energy is that which is spent, often in a subconscious way, hoping that you will finally meet the kind of person in whom you could be interested. If you had your mind set on an important job promotion within a certain number of years, you would be concerned with your performance on any minor or major task along the way. Similarly with your personal life. For those who are interested in settling down with someone, it's like a major developmental task—a promotion. In other words, your desires and hopes are not simply abstract motivations that you activate on occasion, but are emotional drives that are the backdrop to many of your everyday thoughts and activities. This kind of energy is probably the most difficult to measure since it is part and parcel of your being until its function has been served.

Specific mental energy is more focused and deliberate. It is the kind of energy that you might spend trying to optimize your chances of meeting someone through your ordinary everyday activities, such as shopping or doing the laundry—what we refer to as private strategies. Janet, a thirty-nine-year-old travel agent, confided that she is not very spontaneous anymore about when and where she carries out her errands. In describing her weekly trip to the local Pathmark, Janet told us, "It's not that I completely change what I'm going to do on any given day, but I do make slight alterations. For example, I'm an early riser—even on weekends. Part of me would like to get my grocery shopping done at eight in the morning—I don't have to hassle with all the people and then I have the rest of the day to do more fun things. But I decided I won't go—because I feel that I have to try and be around more people if I'm ever going to meet someone, and an empty grocery store is not the answer."

While it may not compare to a workout on the Nautilus equipment, involvement in the search for a mate also requires considerable physical energy, which like mental energy, can be broken down into the general and the specific. General physical energy is what many singles described to us as the feeling of being "on." Like other species of animals, humans display ritualized behaviors when involved in courtship and flirtation. When a woman or man enters a crowded singles bar, noticeable changes occur: slight alterations in posture, increased facial expressions, hair primping, eye movements, changes that are registered by your body and ultimately expend energy. These kinds of adjustments are constantly being made whenever the situation becomes defined as one in which you want to attract someone's attention or respond in a flirtatious manner.

When we observed interactions at singles bars, flirtatious

behaviors between men and women were only part of the picture. In singles bars, even the interactions between people of the same sex are energy laden. Why? Because there are hidden dimensions to the interactions that reflect people's expectations for appropriate behavior—or what sociologists refer to as role playing. It was amazing to watch the transformation in people—women, in particular—as they entered the bars. It was almost as though they were each told some incredibly funny joke as they stepped over the threshold. Groups of two or three women friends would enter the bar and almost immediately become filled with laughter, complete with facial and gestural expression.

There is really nothing mysterious or devious about these behaviors. They merely reflect the belief (of women) that men are more attracted to women who can have a good time and do not appear weighed down with problems. This is not to say that women friends do not sincerely have a fun time when they go out together, but rather that by going to a singles bar one is participating in shared beliefs of what is appropriate behavior. Perhaps what some people describe as the artificiality of singles bars is derived from feeling that only a small slice of a person's personality is ever being exposed—that part which is programmed for fun. Nonetheless, the generalized energy that is expended can be substantial. As Tina, a twenty-nine-year-old stockbroker, put it, "It's like all of my senses are working at one time. I'm engaged in a conversation, but listening to those around me, aware of everyone in my line of sight and noticing if they're aware of me, taking walks to the bathroom or to the bar at opportune times if I particularly want someone to notice me. By the end of the evening, I'm exhausted." Generalized physical energy occurs almost automatically when you define the situation as one involving attraction or potential attraction. This could occur in a bar, or in any other situation or environment such as walking down a crowded street or sitting in a restaurant.

Specific physical energy is more restricted to those activities or behaviors in which you choose to engage such as grooming, dressing, or preparing for an evening on the town. Although these are activities that are practiced by everyone, not just singles, singles are more likely to focus on appearance-related behaviors than those who are not interested in meeting someone of the opposite sex.

Why did Joan focus so much on the idea of "energy" when we interviewed her? Let's face it, for someone in a serious relationship or who is married, doing the laundry, or shopping for food or clothes is simply that. There is no hidden agenda or need for special primping other than what you would ordinarily do. This is not to imply that a Dr. Jekyll–Mr. Hyde transformation accompanies an "I do," but only to suggest that when you are not interested in meeting someone of the opposite sex, there is less relative energy expended on appearance and less awareness of or response to flirtatious signals from the men or women around you.

Why Women Look and Men Don't

At this point you are probably asking yourself why we haven't written about the private strategies of men. The apparent bias in this chapter also bothered us, to the point that we reexamined the data from our focus groups and personal interviews. What we came up with was the unsettling conclusion that private strategies appear to be more characteristic of women's behavior than men's. Now, to two female sociologists, one of whom came of age during the women's movement, some explanation was necessary.

There is ample reference in the literature on gender differences to support the fact that woman, not man, is the more social animal. Carol Gilligan, in her book entitled *A Different Voice,* demonstrates how men and women have different orientations to the world around them. Women focus on attachments and social relationships, men on autonomy. Some were in the middle of a long conversation. He asked me in for a glass of wine. Actually I didn't go in; we sat on his porch and talked for a couple of hours. It was dark by the time I left and he insisted on walking me home. A year and a half later, we were married."

Amy told us, "If I was trying to advise someone, I would tell them to take a good look around, at the places they are right now. It's too easy to get so wrapped up in your own concerns you miss what's right in front of you. I almost did."

I'll See You at the Office

In chapter 1 we made the point that the structures that once enabled men and women to meet, in a relatively smooth and painless way, are no longer doing their job. In the search for new places and new structures, some are looking again to the workplace.

Companies that once scowled over "fraternization" are having second thoughts. A marketing manager observed, "If we spend all our time here, where else are we supposed to meet?"

A personnel director for a major corporation told us, "It's no surprise that companies are basically interested in what's good for *them*. We used to look for solid family men, because they wouldn't have a lot of distractions. By the same token, we didn't want office flirtations that might wreck a marriage. Things are different now because there are so many more unmarried professionals in the workplace, especially talented single women. The image of the boss and the secretary doesn't hold anymore; these days it's more likely to be 'manager to manager.' We can't stop them from meeting each other."

Rosalind, a twenty-nine-year-old internal auditor, met her husband in the course of a routine audit of his department: "I had seen him in the elevator before, but our company is so huge, you really only know a few of the people. When I saw him in the elevator after the audit, he would nod and say hello. When we met in the cafeteria a few times, he came over and sat with me. We really got to know each other gradually, over two or three months, before he asked me out."

The office bears a faint resemblance to the classroom as a possible meeting place, since the reason for being there is not specifically to meet, and the routine activity you are engaged in allows observation and light socialization, without the commitment of a date.

When it comes to ranking workplaces as meeting places, a lot depends on the specifics. A second-grade school teacher does not tend to meet many eligibles in the course of a workday; neither do the many people employed in small offices. Even in a large corporation, those around you may all be married, or the wrong age or sex. And don't forget that some companies still have a tacit policy against employees dating, or have rules against employing more than one member of a family, in case you're contemplating marriage.

Nevertheless, that still leaves endless possibilities in the comings, goings, and lunch hours of a typical workday. People reported they had met their mates "on the subway," "riding the bus," "in a limo on the way to the airport," and "on the Staten Island Ferry." One woman told us she met her husband on the way to work when he rear-ended her BMW on the expressway.

An additional aspect of meeting through the workplace is the fact that companies frequently deal with other companies. Mike, a forty-two-year-old corporate manager, met his wife through a focused group video tape: "She's a consultant who leads group discussions with housewives, on products like ours, and analyzes the market implications of what they say. The first time I saw her on tape, I wanted to meet her; she has a real talent with people and that came through. When she came back for her presentation, I made sure I was there."

What is the best way to meet someone? What is the best place? Without meaning to be glib, we could answer that the best way is the way that works, and the best place is any place at all.

Thinking Positive

Among the successful ways of meeting, methods fall into the categories of either direct or indirect. We've already discussed many of the direct ways people have met. The indirect are more difficult to isolate because they frequently involve a certain attitude, rather than an activity.

There is a story about a woman in her sixties whose husband had died the previous year. They had been very close, and their daily life patterns were so interwoven that the woman suffered greatly from loneliness. In addition, she viewed the future without hope. She told her friend, "I'm sixty-two years old. There are widows all around me. I want to be married, but I know it is hopeless." Her friend told her nothing was hopeless; if that was what she wanted, all she needed to do was to tell herself every day that what she wanted was to find a good man and to marry him. Her friend said that whenever the thought came to her during the day, she should repeat her goal to herself.

The woman did as suggested. Days went by, and weeks, until finally six months had passed. One day when she was at the drugstore having a prescription filled, the pharmacist, who was also in his sixties, mentioned he did not like to see the holidays approach since his wife had died. After that, whenever the woman had her prescriptions filled, they would talk. One day he invited her to a concert; then she invited him for dinner. There were more concerts, and more dinners, and by the end of the year they were married. She says it was all due to the power of positive thinking. He says it was because of her high blood pressure (and her need for prescription medicine).

This example demonstrates the importance of an open at-

149

titude and a firm conviction about what you want. People who are clear about goals seem to be more adept at noticing opportunities, entering conversations, and converting the most casual encounters into potential dates.

Annie, a journalist, told us she once had a five-year plan for marriage. Divorced at thirty-five, she decided she wanted to learn how to be single before entering into another marriage: "I had lived at home until I married my first husband. I've never had any experience being totally on my own. I felt I needed that; otherwise I could never be sure if I was marrying again for emotional or financial security. I didn't want to marry someone because I had some question about making it on my own."

At the time of the interview, Annie told us, "You know what they say about 'the best laid plans.' I did fine for nearly three years and then I met Jack. It was either scrap the plan or lose him, because for him the timing was right. I thought, 'Hey, I can adapt.' I really had not planned on any serious dating for five years. It had taken almost two to put a messy divorce totally to rest, and I wanted a time-out before any other involvements. But men kept asking me out. Friends would say, 'It's not fair. You don't care, and you're the one who has all these guys around.' It was true, and I found that rather odd because I wasn't any different from my friends—except in one respect. I really wasn't looking for anybody. And frankly, I think that was it. I was up-front about wanting to develop *friendships*. I've always liked men in my life. I like to be around them. I like their point of view; they help me keep a certain balance. But it was strictly friendship that I wanted, and I was very clear about that. I figure friendship is always the best beginning anyway. Let things develop from there. That's how Jack and I started out."

The last two women appeared to find husbands without making any effort at all. One might say there wasn't any strategy, that it was pure luck. We would argue that it wasn't luck: The attitude was the strategy, a spontaneous reaching out, instead of closing in.

Attitude is both subtle and powerfully present. None of us like to feel we are being judged; but we ourselves judge and are constantly being judged. Have you ever passed someone on the street and something about them—they look so pleasant—makes you want to smile? On the other hand, we steer clear of the thunderclouds in our midst.

In some ways attitude is the most difficult strategy of all, because you can't fake it. If you really dislike women, or men, if you are highly judgmental when it comes to their respective foibles, it's difficult to hide.

Related to attitude is the goal of making friends who are of the opposite sex and keeping them. One woman told us, "You don't have to see a man as a potential husband to stay friends with him. You just never know what the future will bring. You may be determined to stay single at one point, and by the next year something could change. You don't have to know the end of the story before it even begins."

Christine, a forty-nine-year-old pediatrics nurse, agreed to have dinner with Matthew, an old friend, during a visit to her home town: "I had not been back for fifteen years. He and his wife had both been friends of mine. I didn't have a chance to see them much, but we exchanged Christmas cards over the years. Sally was killed in an auto accident two years ago, but I still kept sending Christmas cards to Matthew. I would have never thought of him as a husband because he was married most of the time I knew him, but when we went to dinner that night, things were totally different. He says he felt it right away. He tells me, 'I fell in love over the shrimp cocktail.' "

Cara, a twenty-eight-year-old pharmacist, also became reacquainted after a number of years, with the man who was to become her husband. She told us, "It was at our ten-year high school reunion. I almost didn't go. I liked high school and the friends I made there, but it seemed such a long time ago. Anyway, some of the guys I knew before were still single. The nice thing was their memories of me were good—I was always pretty straightforward with people, even when

151

we were breaking up. I had dated John a few times, and at the reunion he asked me if it was okay for him to call. A few days later he did; we started seeing each other again, and that was it."

Know Thyself—The Fundamental Chord

A few years ago, Laurel was a successful, thirty-four-year-old publicist for an ad agency. She had dated more men than she cared to think about, and still had not found anyone she was willing to spend the rest of her life with: "I was seriously considering how to prepare myself for not marrying at all. On the one hand, there were hundreds of people who could have been compatible, who had similar education, skills, background. But one of the things I know about myself is that similarity would not have been enough. There is a part of me that doesn't often show, but it's always there and it needs to be addressed. It's a certain sense of awe about all the beautiful things I see. If someone doesn't have that—if they just say, 'Yeah, the sunset looks great,' but it doesn't dazzle them—they wouldn't really like the best part of me.

"When I met Marty, I had just about given up on ever finding that. I was thinking what it would be like to scrap the idea of ever having a child, and to think about spending all of my life alone. I was sitting by the lake reading, when I felt someone there, and looked up. This guy had stopped his bike and said, 'If you really want to see something incredible, look over there.' I turned around and there were all these thunderclouds gathering, with light streaming down through them. It was breathtaking. We both just looked at them. After a while we began to talk.... It was so natural. He asked for my phone number and we started going out. I think we both knew from that first time we were right for each other." Laurel has since married Marty, and they are the proud parents of a thirteen-month-old baby girl.

In this case we wanted to talk to Marty also, to see what

the counterpart of that special chord might be from the male point of view. Marty teaches in the humanities department of a small local college. He told us when he saw Laurel by the lake, "There was something about her that looked as though she belonged there. I've gotten very good at spotting that quality; maybe because I know what the opposite looks like." He told us about one of his first loves when he was twenty-three: "We built a fire on the beach...I opened a bottle of wine. It was very romantic. When we were walking, I had picked up a really great piece of driftwood to take back to my apartment. I showed it to her, and pointed out some of the special shape. I'll never forget it. She took it in her hands, agreed that it was really a terrific-looking piece of wood—and put it on the fire. Needless to say, that was not the girl for me."

Singles who are aware that there is a strong guiding principle in their lives need to listen to that in the same way as those who march to the beat of a different drummer need to listen. As individuals with unusual hopes or expectations told us over and over, you have no choice but to hold out for them.

Kate grew up on a ranch near El Paso. Despite the fact that she was educated at exclusive eastern colleges and encouraged to pursue a career in interior design, her first love has always been horses. She was given a pony when she could scarcely walk. Because playmates were rare, she spent most of her free time at the stables, riding and grooming the horses.

"You learn how they think, and act. There's an honesty about them you don't find in most people. When my favorite horse, Rajah, was killed in a rock slide, it was like losing a person. Most people have no idea how you could possibly feel that way about a horse. I've had a lot of relationships that didn't work out, and one of the reasons is they never understood that essential thing about me. When I first saw Tim's sketches, I knew he really understood horses: the way

153

they hold their heads, their expressions, the muscular tension. He could see it. I wrote him a fan letter. We started to correspond. Tim grew up on a dairy farm in Wisconsin, but they had always kept a few horses. We compared our childhood horse stories. By the time we met, I was already in love. He told me he had felt the same way. We were married just three months later."

It is sometimes said that "half of success is really wanting it." You might object that most of the singles in this chapter just lucked out, that if you were fortunate enough to have been on that hike, or at that mailbox, or in that particular club, you would have found someone by now, too. In one sense you are right; these former singles are not that different from you, except in one way: They have learned to utilize an array of key factors in their search for that special relationship.

Summing Up—Points for Pondering

Doubling up The art of parsimony. A major feature of successful singles was that, whenever possible, they combined the search for a relationship with another activity. Whether they were theater buffs or nature lovers, whether the activity was taking a class or going shopping, if it could be done at a time or place that increased the chance of meeting other singles, that was when they did it. Obviously this is not always possible. We do not recommend advertising for Mr./Ms. Right in the same space where you're trying to sell a stereo.

Learning from your mistakes Everyone makes mistakes. The crucial factor is how you deal with them. If you go for a walk in the country and are drenched in a sudden storm, you can either vow never to take another walk or decide next time you will bring an umbrella. The worst thing you can do if a strategy doesn't work is to forget about it—at least before you analyze what went wrong. It's a little like the guy who ate a gumdrop just before getting the flu when he was nine, and hasn't touched a gumdrop since.

Giving yourself a break   Life may not always be a bed of roses, but no one ever said it had to be a thicket of thorns either. Before taking another step in your search for that special someone, examine the components of your average day. Analyze your two most frequented settings: the place where you live and the place where you work. Why launch energy-consuming strategies before arranging for a daily setting that maximizes your opportunities to meet someone? Although we do not advise quitting your job or running out on your lease, we do suggest that when the time comes to make a move on either front, you keep the demographics in mind.

Being realistic   An attitude of mind. Although this also relates to saving time, it primarily involves a sense of awareness; a counterpart to "street smarts," which might be called "singles smarts." Singles who appeared most successful in meeting and dating followed these precepts:

• Know when to cut your losses. If you're looking for a permanent relationship and you suddenly realize he/she is afraid of intimacy, bite the bullet and move on.

• Don't seek composites. Everyone loves variety, but if you are looking for a homebody, don't expect that person to double as the life of everyone's party. People cannot be themselves and their opposites at the same time. If you're seeking someone who is ambitious and self-directed, it isn't fair to expect that person also to be charmingly self-effacing with a heavy dose of dependence—on you.

• Make sure your expectations are realistic. That does not mean lowering your standards, but it does mean making sure they reflect your true priorities. We've all heard a lot about singles being too picky. But what does that mean? For women, it has often been associated with the "knight in shining armor" image. We do not advise discarding that image any more than we advise single men to throw out their image of the ideal partner. But we do recommend a reassessment to see if it has kept pace with your adult hopes and dreams. The fantasy part of the knight or lady, imbedded in infatuation, can be scrapped without a second thought. But those aspects of your ideal partner that are based on valued characteristics and traits essential to your view of the world at its best are worth holding out for; they not only represent what you want but embody the best you have to offer.

Persistence pays off Our final observation is that successful singles, those who found that special someone, refused to accept singlehood gracefully. For them, the game wasn't over until they decided to quit. If the last strategy didn't work, they would try it again, or try something else. But they were determined to secure the kind of relationship they wanted; and they did.

9

A Look into the Future

The time has come, the Walrus said, to talk of many things; of shoes and ships and sealing wax, of cabbages and kings...

Lewis Carroll

Our look into the future begins with a glimpse into the past. Think for a moment of your grandparents. Most likely they were married until one of them died. You may cherish childhood memories of grandma in her apron baking cookies, grandpa puttering in the back yard; or you may remember instead that grandma and grandpa yelled at each other a lot; that grandpa would slam the door after an argument and hole up in the basement with his woodworking tools and a bottle of Jack Daniel's. It hardly sounds like traditional marital bliss. So why did they put up with it... and with each other? There were three major factors (outside of religious beliefs and social consequences) that contributed to the enduring marriages of our grandparents.

Factor One—It Can't Last Forever

A few generations ago, husband and wife were more likely to wait it out, a strategy that refers to both the individual argument and the long-term marriage. This may not have been due as much to moral fiber as it was to the issue of life expectancy. Only a few short decades ago, life expectancy for women was age seventy-two, while for men it was age sixty-six. But no one needed to know those statistics. All

157

they needed to do was look around and note the number of men who died in their fifties or a few days after retirement to realize a bad marriage wasn't going to last forever. Also, for those who made it to an older age, the tendency toward multiple health problems placed the emphasis on survival rather than quality of life.

Factor Two—His and Hers

Family planning, along with better methods of birth control and changing expectations for women, now means the last child leaves home while both parents are still relatively young. This not only has dramatic effects on the mother of the family, but on the father as well. "Hers" is the much-publicized "empty nest syndrome," while "his" is the almost equally publicized "male menopause." Some would argue that both are a fiction of sorts, that the empty nest is just another life stage that women generally welcome as a time to develop old or new-found interests, while male menopause is just another version of the "seven-year itch" with a pseudomedical explanation. (The continued decrease in the male production of testosterone over the years is more akin to gradual aging than to the abrupt changes of menopause.)

Nonetheless, the two are interrelated. Once her nest was empty, he could afford his menopause, in the same way students can afford to get sick once final exams are over. All of us are capable of astonishing effort when the situation requires it. We would argue that the progressive lack of demands as the modern family ages allows both men and women the luxury of considering starting life anew. One woman told us, "My grandmother had ten kids. She was too busy baking half a dozen loaves of bread a day to think much about empty nests." That may not be the perfect solution to ensuring a long-lasting marriage, but it does remind us that people operate within the constraints of their environment. In examining change, we need to look at how that environment supports or suppresses the move toward change.

Factor Three—Knowing Your Options

If you think you want to make a job change, how do you go about it? For most people, high on the list is checking out your options. The goal is to follow that sage advice, "Never quit one job until you have another." If you have a terrific job offer and are bored with what you are doing, you most likely will make a move. If, on the other hand, you hate your job, but those available are worse, you probably won't rock the employment boat.

For those who are married, the options have changed. Women who are able to earn their own living no longer find it necessary to stay married to husbands who are alcoholic, abusive, or overly demanding. The fact that they are economically independent may also raise the requirements for staying married; the ease of "going it alone" means even minor infractions or incompatabilities could end in divorce today.

For a husband in years past, it wasn't his economics that kept a trying marriage together, but hers. If she didn't have any alternatives for supporting herself and maintaining a home, especially where children were involved, he couldn't afford a divorce.

The fact that men are still keenly aware of those economics was frequently evidenced in our interviews. We were told, especially by those men under forty, that a major requirement for a marriage partner was that she have some profession or means of support to ensure that "I'm not stuck paying for her if things don't work out."

The Psychology of Change

"The whole world is going to hell in a hand-basket" was an observation often used by an older generation to register displeasure with the larger social system. Complaints about the current state of affairs have most likely been around as long as language itself. And they have probably always been stated in ways that exempt the speaker. It is always *they* who have screwed things up.

At the heart of this issue is the question of the individual vs. the larger social group. We have seen rapid changes enacted by individuals in courtship and marriage in the last twenty years, and we have heard numerous complaints about those changes—often from the very people who were most vocal in supporting them. It's a little like the classic fairy tale of the three wishes: The first is usually wasted; the second is fulfilled; and the third is used to undo the second, which did not turn out quite the way the wisher had envisioned (e.g., King Midas's daughter was turned into gold).

For society, the doing and the undoing constitute an ongoing process. This does not mean it is painless, or without serious consequences—especially for those caught in periods of change. In one sense we are all part of a huge, on-going social experiment: If it works, we'll keep it; if not, there will be adjustment and change.

A major impetus to change occurs when people simply do not like what is going on. Currently we are experiencing some of the long-term results of changes in the ways men and women relate to each other, and they are telling us they do not like what they see. Complaints, across the board, outweighed any perceived benefits. The nature of complaints varied with age groups, but mass dissatisfaction was apparent in all of them.

Cecily, a fifty-seven-year-old fundraiser, lamented what she called the general "lack of style" in the way men and women approach each other today. She told us, "When I was ten, my parents sent me to dancing school. We would line up across from these angelic-looking little boys who would bow and ask us to dance. We were at the age where little boys and little girls would have preferred throwing rocks at each other, but we were still taught the correct way to behave. No one tries to teach them anything today; by sixth grade they may have gone to bed already—without ever having had that first dance; something is very wrong—and it's very sad."

Trudy, a thirty-four-year-old mother of two, expressed bitterness. She told us, "Whoever started this has a lot to answer for. I don't know if it was women's lib, or if men were just being opportunists, but now it's chaos. I never wanted to be divorced; I never expected to be. But somewhere along the way the rules changed and nobody told me." Her husband had walked out of a twelve-year-old marriage by leaving a note on the dining room table and an envelope with fifty dollars. "I didn't even know there was anything wrong. He was a little more irritable just before it happened, but he said that was because of his job. As soon as the divorce was final, he married his twenty-three-year-old secretary. The hardest thing was that he acted as though it was okay."

But men were not the only ones who walked out. Roland, a forty-one-year-old allergist, told us he came home one night to find a babysitter with the kids and a note from his wife saying she needed a life of her own: "I couldn't believe it. She just packed her things one day and left. She didn't even want the kids. At first I thought it must be another guy, but it wasn't. She just did not want the responsibility anymore. So I'm raising the kids, and she still got half of everything. There's something screwy about that."

A major force deeply affecting individuals and their relationships today has been the growing emphasis on autonomy. The positive aspect of autonomy is that society dictates as little of your behavior as possible. You are respected as an individual, free to shape your life as creatively as you wish. The down side is you have few role models and little positive support for those roles you undertake.

Autonomy is always at war with forceful majorities. But ironically, autonomy becomes widespread only when it is a value supported and reinforced by the larger group. When the larger group is too successful and autonomy threatens to undermine group values, a certain chaos erupts while the age-old tug-of-war, between the individual good and that of the majority, is reestablished.

What has been the effect of autonomy on the issue of singles meeting each other and entering into relationships? Although few men or women would admit to favoring *dependence* in a relationship, it has become more and more apparent that a relationship between two totally *independent* people quickly develops into no relationship at all.

Men and women today are beginning to take a second look at the golden idol of independence, and are protesting that autonomy isn't worth the price. We hear growing use of the term "interdependence," which is used to describe two basically independent people who have chosen to entwine their lives. This, of course, calls for a certain bending of the total autonomy rules. You still must be basically independent, but you can depend *a little* on your special person, assuming that person depends *a little* on you as well.

One man commented, "That's the dumbest thing I ever heard. Not that you mutually depend on each other, but the fact that there's a word for it. That used to be what was expected in any good relationship."

His point is thought-provoking. Why do we need fancy new words for solid old concepts? In the sciences, mathematical formulas proliferate as our knowledge of the universe expands and we need more precise measures to conduct an analysis. In the social sciences, as we examine new social developments and more complex patterns of relationships, we also need more precise terms in order to adequately describe and analyze them.

Changes and Readjustments

Karla, a twenty-nine-year-old accountant, expressed annoyance over what she called "male whining," in their com-

plaints about women. She told us, "Men are going to have to accept something they didn't have to accept ten or fifteen years ago. They're having to adjust to the equality of women and the aggressiveness of women, and they can't stand it."

One of the problems with such a discussion is that equality is not defined; often it is used to refer to a political and economic position, as well as interpersonal relationships. Most of the men we interviewed did not express resentment over equality for women in the public sector. It was in private relationships, where they were uncertain what equality was supposed to mean, that it created problems for them. Add to this the fact that equality can be interpreted by women according to their own personality style, and the confusion is magnified. The concept of equality takes on so many meanings that it fails to have any meaning at all and becomes, instead, a red flag in any male-female discussion.

In today's world, rationality tops the list of best traits. If your emotions are showing, you're perceived as "losing it." We are advised, "Don't get mad, get even." But what happens when the nature of an interaction is, of itself, an emotional one?

One man told us how his latest relationship had ended. He and his "significant other" were sitting on the couch in his living room, after a romantic dinner for two. She wanted him to do the dishes before they settled down in front of the fireplace for the evening.

"I told her I would rather leave the kitchen stuff for morning and spend the time with her. That was all I said. She immediately started ranting about 'the double standard,' and how men could get away with being slobs, but women had to conform to other people's rules. She turned a great evening into the battle of the sexes. I've seen other women do that. It really turns me off. I didn't get around to telling her this, but the irony is, it was my mother who taught me to leave party dishes for morning. It's true. She used to stack them out of sight in the oven until the next day. She always said, the dishes can wait; people can't."

Emotions that accompany relationships between men and women tend to be highly volatile: Love, passion, jealousy—sometimes hatred—may be present in any combination. But under the mandate of rationality, these strong feelings are often expressed in code. The rhetoric of equality for women may, in the hands of an angry female, turn into verbal male-bashing that has little to do with feminism. At the same time, a man with an especially assertive woman may find himself sniping at a movement when his real target is the behavior of one specific person. As one thirty-two-year-old office manager told us, "I don't mind a good old-fashioned fight; I would just like to know when I'm in one."

When the Hite report appeared recently, the media jumped on juicy reports that women are secretly furious with men, that there will never be a truce in the battle of the sexes, and that if men only knew how women really felt, they would tremble in their Guccis and head for the nearest monastery.

Although the sampling frame of the report has been severely criticized, the findings have been publicized over and over, and the book was an instant bestseller. In our opinion, despite the lack of a representative sample, there is a ring of truth in the powerful sense of rage expressed by Hite's respondents. It was as though after a hard climb women looked around and discovered that instead of a pot of gold at the end of the rainbow, there was just another mountain.

In the sexual arena, the freedom that women expected would give them greater equality backfired. Allowing men the option of sex with the nice girl they may or may not wind up marrying increased the male tendency to drag their feet on the way to the license bureau, while females could not escape the imperative of their biological clock.

Added to their frustration were economic realities.

Women have heard the rhetoric of equal pay and economic freedom, but are not experiencing it. Few people would call earning scarcely enough money to keep body and soul together economic independence; yet for many women, especially heads of households, that is the case.

Just as both men and women have become disillusioned with sexual freedom, women are finding that the world of work isn't quite what they had expected. The end result, economic independence, is undeniably a good one. But what falls in between—the constant struggle to prove competence, being shut out of the male network (which impedes career climbs), the difficulty of finding female mentors—has proven for many to be far more exhausting than they ever anticipated.

No wonder Hite's women are angry. Success in the world of work generally means women must put more effort into it than men. If they are considering marriage, they are faced with an uncertain future: Either do one job at a time, which means staying home to raise the kids, or do two jobs at a time, which means tending hearth and home while battling the briefcase world on a daily basis. It's possible, but tough.

For women who may prefer to be homemakers, the option has essentially disappeared. The political reality is that as long as divorce exists on a large scale, and as long as women still tend to raise the children, they face a very real possibility of poverty, unless they cover their bets with a profession. Perhaps part of the anger on the part of women is knowing they must now do this, whether they want to or not, to secure their future.

In general, we did not find men were hostile to the goals of women, but that they simply lacked an understanding of issues with which they had no experience. A typical attitude was that expressed by one thirty-seven-year-old manager, who told us, "Women wanted to be sexually aggressive; they did it. They wanted to be professionals; they did it. But they still aren't satisfied. I have no idea what women want now.

Whatever it is, give it to them. I just don't want to hear about it anymore."

The point is not who is right and who is wrong, but rather that the transitions men and women have undergone have sometimes led them to stand back and view each other as invading forces. Few generations have had to weather the extreme changes we have seen in sex roles and relationships in the past twenty years.

We are now in the midst of a period of readjustment and reevaluation. As more extreme positions gravitate toward the mean, men and women will again be able to view each other as friends and lovers, but with a deeper understanding of the unique problems and viewpoints of both sexes.

Meeting—You're on Your Own

Singles who are meeting and dating today are often reluctant pioneers in an environment the last generation never had to face. We generally get our ideas about major transitions from our parents. They ease the way on that first day of school with the promise of a special treat and the reassurance that they will be there at the last bell. When you're ready to hunt for that first job, they are there with advice and emotional support. But when you're ready to look for dating partners, you are suddenly on your own. If you should be given any advice, it seems hopelessly outdated, perhaps even silly; but most likely the topic is sheathed in silence. Parents do not know what to tell you, because for them, "meeting" was something that just naturally happened.

We have already discussed the structures that once accomplished the task of singles meeting singles. People who grew up when these structures were operating simply do not know what to suggest to singles today. In fact, some of the currently recommended methods would have been taboo thirty years ago. In the fifties, a woman who engaged in

conversation with a man she didn't know would be considered nothing more than a pickup. Today, women are advised to use any and every opportunity to meet new men: the supermarket checkout line, the airport, hailing a cab, buying a shirt. The advice is, "Be friendly," "Strike up a conversation." But unlike the job interview, they won't get any coaching at home on how to engage in these public encounters.

To complicate matters, both men and women carry around some of the old parental attitudes about the propriety of ways to meet. Even while trying to engage in new methods, they experience a sense of uneasiness about their legitimacy. This is magnified by a certain lack of clarity: Just because you engage in public conversation does not mean all the stops are out, that you have no sense of morals or moral behavior. It means only what it appears to mean: that, in lieu of formal structures, it is one of the many informal methods singles engage in to meet.

The big question for the future is: Will singles be obliged to continue to engineer meeting each other on their own, or can we expect to see the development of new structures to replace the old? Our answer is an emphatic "That depends." We know there will continue to be change, but the form of that change depends on responses made by both individuals and institutions. For example, although it is unlikely church attendance among singles will increase in the near future, many churches today are attempting to address the needs of singles by providing meeting rooms for those groups.

In the case of family, although there has been a slight trend for singles to temporarily move back with families, particularly in cases of financial setbacks, the internal family organization, imbedded in geographic stability and lifelong membership, can no longer be taken for granted. You may move back home to find yourself in the midst of a blended family, in a different neighborhood, perhaps even in a different state.

As for schools, it is unlikely there will be any massive return to the classroom as matchmaker, not only because people are frequently delaying marriage until their education is behind them, but because of the increasing number of singles over thirty.

This means that singles will have to adapt to the idea that it is up to them to meet someone. Although we may see the emergence of some new methods to routinize meeting, such as the personal ads, those methods will still have to be activated by the individual. The shift from public to personal responsibility in finding someone is a permanent one.

Dating—The All-American Pastime

In the past, numerous studies in sociology and psychology have dealt primarily with dating, courtship, and mate selection. But the ambiguity and lack of structure of dating in the 1980s has made empirical studies increasingly difficult. It is no longer accurate to assume the major function of dating is to find a marriage partner, or that dating occurs primarily in the under-thirty age group or mostly among people who have never been married.

Today the old-fashioned date is only one possible category of dating: He calls her, invites her to go out with him, and if she accepts, he expects to pick her up at her home, and to pay for the evening's expenses. Add to this the implied possibility for romance and you have the ingredients of the classic old-fashioned date. In the past, a key factor in this interaction was the shared definition of dating. It was this consensus of meaning that made it so awkward if you were required to take your pretty cousin to the senior prom, or let your mother fix you up with the son of her best friend. It was this pretense of a date, when the ingredients were not quite authentic, that young people found intolerable. True, there was some excuse; these last-resort tactics were generally reserved for those special events viewed (usually by one's parents) as critical to a well-rounded high school or college experience. But they also were seen by participants as a violation of dating norms, a shared perception that is possible only when everyone knows the way it is *supposed to be.*

In examining dating today, the norms are far less clear, the elements more difficult to separate out. The old-fashioned date is still easy enough to identify, but today there is, in addition, a whole typology of dating. At the very beginning of the social event, there is no set model. For example, if you go back to the original definition of a date, what happens if *she* does the asking? Is it still a date? Is she then supposed to go to his house and escort him, and is it assumed that she pays any expenses incurred for the evening's entertainment?

Singles told us the *least* problematic issue is who escorts whom. As one woman noted, "You have to use a little common sense. Sometimes it's just more convenient to meet somewhere." But what was very problematic was the question of picking up the tab. If she asks, can it be assumed that she pays? Most singles responded with a resounding "yes," but there are still enough exceptions to make the situation less than predictable.

Jim, a thirty-year-old CPA, told us a woman he had dated several times called him up and invited him out for dinner at a popular restaurant: "I was flattered, and thought it was really nice. Then the bill came. I'm not comfortable having women pay for things, but I didn't want to make a big deal out of it either, so I just said, 'Why don't we split this?' Was I in for a surprise! She was outraged. She yelled, 'I never pay for anything when I go out with a man.' I said to her, 'Look, you were the one who asked me out for dinner.' She was really angry. She paid her half of the bill and stormed out of the restaurant. That was it. I never saw her again. I didn't call her and she didn't call me."

Incidents like this both mirror and add to the confusion of understanding the current norms and expectations for dating today. Our book can't solve the problems of diverse expectations in dating, but we can prepare you for some of what you may encounter.

The issue of who pays for a date has become increasingly sensitive, not because we have all turned miserly, but because of the underlying meaning attached to it. When dating was a prelude to courtship, men were investing in a wife in the same way they invested in four years of college. Although they may have had a few false starts, the date was, in general, an investment in the future. However, since dating has become an end in itself, a man could spend years paying costly "doubles" before ever getting married.

For many women, it is this awareness that underlies the adamant insistence to pay their own way. In the fifties the man paid for the woman and both parties knew it didn't give him any right to take liberties. Today, the woman may wonder if she indeed "owes" him something for that evening at the theater, and he in turn may think she does. The problem is that women who insist on paying without considering each situation on its own merits may reinforce a perceived relationship between paying and power.

A wealthy widow in her sixties, who dated a man of very modest means, told us, "I would never insult John by paying for things. I do love the symphony, however, so for his birthday I gave him two season tickets."

Because money has so many different meanings for different people, from matters of simple courtesy to buying sexual favors, and because there is no uniformity in dating expectations today, you may find it necessary to be more direct. It is not a comfortable topic, but it is a lot better to talk about who pays than to sabotage a relationship because of false assumptions.

TV Tribalism—The New Teachers

"Tell me who your friends are and I'll tell you who you are." This bit of conventional wisdom speaks to the broader issue of values. The underlying question is: How did you get to be the way you are? The answer is: You were taught, not only by what you were told but by observation and imitation.

In the simplest of societies, socialization tends to be uniform and predictable. Primitive tribes find it easy to transmit cultural beliefs since most learning remains within the bounds of a relatively small group. A child is taught the same behavior and value expectations by other members of the tribe, as by parents or peers.

But once a society becomes more complex, multitiered and multistructured, the socialization process also becomes increasingly complex. Although the family is viewed as the primary socializing agent, once the child enters school, that system along with peer groups, exerts a powerful new influence. Parents begin to hear things like, "Jeff's mother said he could," for everything from riding the merry-go-round to flushing away the goldfish.

The influence of school and peer groups has long been taken for granted; but few anticipated the rise of television as a major socializing agent. In its early stages, parents worried over warnings by the "experts" that too much TV would turn their kids' brains into spaghetti. But as they themselves increased their attachment to the tube, and discovered its great baby-sitting potential, parents as well as kids began to absorb the cultural models presented via satellite.

At the same time individuals heard the tenets of sexual freedom articulated from a quasi-political point of view, they were seeing it glamorized on TV, especially the nighttime soaps such as "Dallas" and "Dynasty." Couched in terms of wealth and power, the messages of self-indulgence, success linked to exploitation, and sex as a device for manipulation became as much a part of their daily lives as brushing their teeth.

In addition, the models portrayed on TV were more powerful and consistent in their total value system than those presented in most families. They were also more attractive. The values and expectations once transmitted via family have been reduced to a common pop culture shared by TV viewers as in a quasi-tribe.

The problem with TV tribalism is that the values expressed through the media are made to appear both real and workable. But those who have attempted to live their lives according to the cultural standards depicted on TV find they do not work. In our interviews we were constantly aware of the resulting disillusionment. Often bitter accusations were aimed at a vague target that had misled and misinformed.

Individual frustration increases when there is no specific group or person to blame, no one to argue with, no one from whom to get advice or talk things over. Cultural reality becomes a one-way communication system, born anew with each set of TV episodes. It is conceivable that today's singles could become the first generation whose expectations for finding and maintaining relationships are shaped more by TV scriptwriters than by real-life examples. Does this mean your future is irrevocably in the hands of media trendsetters? Only if you permit it to be. One way to escape this cultural trap is simply to be very aware of the powerful influence it exerts on your thinking and expectations. Once you see the emperor *really* has no clothes, it's hard to take him seriously.

A second way is to open your thoughts and values to the scrutiny of peers, which simply means learning to talk things over. One problem with seeking postcollege relationships is that you generally have lost touch with the built-in friendship groups whose members faced the same problems as you did. These groups, which often evaporate on graduation, served as your best advisors. They are not easy to replace; it is difficult to admit you are just as baffled over male/female behavior at thirty or forty as you were at twenty. It's bad enough to admit it to yourself, let alone to those who know you as the competent attorney, office manager, salesperson, or CPA. Yet talking things over is the best way to keep your personal mirror from getting fogged. Not only is it useful for specifics, but it helps give you an accurate reading on what your contemporaries are thinking and feeling—a barometer for comparison.

Trends—Sketching Out Tomorrow

"Stop the world, I want to get off." That line from an old song expresses a common feeling for most of us in times of rapid change. It's a little like watching the scenery from the window of a speeding train. We would like things to stop just long enough for us to get a good look at what is going on.

We may not be able to stop the world, but we can identify the currents that are exerting a constant push and pull on our social world. Before discussing the major trends that we believe will exert the most influence on the nature of relationships in the future, it is important to remember that a trend is only a starting point. It may continue and exert a powerful influence on everyday behavior, or it may only be part of a social readjustment that will decline as further change occurs.

Living Without You

One of the most interesting current trends has been the decrease in cohabitation among singles. For many, the live-in relationship was accepted as a new form of engagement. But instead of merely testing out thoughts and ideas, you could test out housekeeping habits as well. Among the more avant-garde, living together was simply a form of social freedom. If you both wanted to, why not? It was old-fashioned to think in terms of a reputation to protect, and "virgin" was a word that went out with the fifties.

For many, the strong trend away from couples living together prior to marriage has been a surprise development;

not only that, selective sex is making a comeback. Why? One explanation is that women have not found their position improved by a live-in relationship. In fact, studies among college students (a convenient, if not always representative sample) have shown women in a live-in situation tend to enact more stereotypical sex roles. This means they will often do most of the cooking and cleaning, as well as providing sex and paying their fair share of living expenses.

Some argue that the imbalance exists partly because these women are trying to make a good impression. This, added to the fact that statistics show there is no difference in marriage rates between those who have lived together and those who have not, creates a good argument for women to "pass" on cohabitation.

Men, on the other hand, have found live-in arrangements often bring out an unexpected and unwelcome domesticity in their new roommates. One thirty-two-year-old attorney told us, "It wasn't as though she didn't know what I was like. We had been going together for a year. She had stayed over a few weekends. But two weeks after she moved in she was trying to change everything: me, my apartment, my friends. It just wasn't working."

The new conservatism, coupled with a move toward the romantic rather than the sexual, will continue to curtail the number of live-in arrangements. The current view was reflected in the comment of one woman who told us, "The only way I would live with someone is if I had definite wedding plans, a diamond ring in hand. I feel like the old-fashioned father, 'What are your intentions, young man?' I don't have time to fool around ... and I don't want to."

You're Not Getting Older...

A second trend, small but distinct, has had to do with age. *Time* magazine recently featured an article on younger men marrying older women. Other magazines have followed suit.

A few short years ago, older women reported feeling very uneasy in relationships with younger men. They were concerned about social criticism and their own feelings of impropriety. Today, as these relationships become more common, those involved feel less discomfort.

It is difficult to tell how widespread this trend may become, but the basis for relationships between younger men and older women appears solid for both. A fifty-six-year-old anthropologist whose wife had died four years before told us why he stays away from younger women: "Let me give you just one example. One night I was having dinner with a friend in her mid-thirties. We were crossing the street to the restaurant, and she was about to step in a puddle. I took her arm to guide her past it...just a normal gesture. She pulled her arm away and practically shrieked at me, 'I can certainly cross a street without any help!' I was dumbfounded. I don't need to be around women that are so touchy about small gestures. Courtesy never compromised anyone."

A thirty-eight-year-old statistician voiced a similar complaint about women his own age: "Half the time I really don't know what I've said to make a woman lash out. It's like they have a secret list, and if you accidentally say the wrong words, they nail you. I'm not very modern, meaning I don't know what the caveats are. I believe in most of the things women want. They deserve to go after the same jobs, get the same pay, and not have anyone harrass them in the workplace. Sometimes I want to say, 'Hey, if this is how you treat your friends...'

"The woman I'm seeing now is eight years older than I am; she's pretty, she's fun, and she knows who she is. I never hear any of that defensive crap from her, but at the same time, she's very direct, and she gets what she wants, but she does it without making you feel it's part of a vendetta. With younger women I often get the feeling they really want to fight. It's like open warfare. Who needs that?"

The trend of older women with younger men has more

than one explanation. The fact that these women are less threatening is certainly a factor. Another may be that they have "mellowed out." Maybe they were young turks at twenty-five, thirty, or thirty-five, and have learned easier ways to get what they want. Maybe they are no longer struggling up a career ladder, or perhaps they have resigned themselves to working around the system rather than revolutionizing it.

Women have told us one major appeal of younger men is that they understand their need for independence. Also, they are not, as one woman pointed out, "stodgy and in a rut."

Whatever the reasons, older women and younger men are finding rewarding relationships in increasing numbers. One effect of this has been to increase the number of eligibles for women. We noted earlier that when male to female ratios are computed, they're based on the assumption that men will marry same age and younger women, while it has been assumed that women will marry same age and *older* men. As this assumption changes, so do the ratios.

A final word about the age trends: One effect of the publicity on older women dating younger men has been to reinforce for older women feelings of attractiveness and dateability. A few years ago Dr. O'Connor co-authored a study on dating for men and women over age sixty and found dating among the elderly was far more common than most people thought. However, one of the reasons few people were aware of it was that the elderly themselves frequently hid their dating from others, because they feared social censure and ridicule. With age coming out of the closet, the dating climate will be a more comfortable one for them also.

Summing Up

So what does all of this mean? Does the future hold an increasing percentage of single searchers? Will the response be a new, more efficient system of selecting a mate—you can find it in the yellow pages becoming the new norm? Or will the trend be backward? Are the problems of going it alone, coupled with the new conservatism, going to drive people into earlier marriages? Will we replicate the past, where colleges and universities saw diplomas and marriage certificates awarded within weeks of each other?

As sociologists our answer is unequivocal. The social change we are seeing is both fundamental and permanent. We've stepped over the threshold; there is no turning back. New technology, increased divorce rates, and growing economic independence for women are here to stay. To complicate the issue, increased numbers of people will be single (and looking) at *several* periods during their lifetime. This in itself does not mean we have become a society marked by lack of commitment or declining family values, although both may exist.

But it does mean a reevaluation is in order; a realistic assessment of expectations and strategies is the key to finding someone today. Like Alice in *Through the Looking-Glass*, we have stepped into a different world; but unlike Alice, we have some clues to the nature of the terrain.

Epilogue

The problems of singles meeting singles may appear initially to be those of a relatively small but constantly changing group. Men and women are single, they marry, they may or may not become single again or marry again. What does the orderly or disorderly progression of that sector have to do with the rest of us? Plenty. A family begins with (and may remain) a unit of two, the smallest social unit of our society, which forms the base upon which everything else rests.

When the family is threatened in its basic activity of socializing members and sending them off to become part of new families, social order itself is threatened. Does this mean that members who never marry, or divorce, or marry two or three times, are going to cause the world suddenly to blow up? Hardly. But it does mean that if increasing numbers of singles fail to marry, or wind up permanently alone through divorce, the rest of society is going to suffer. Not only will we experience the large-scale psychological effects of unmet intimacy needs, but the rest of us will have to pick up the tab for services the family used to provide routinely.

We tend to take for granted the two key areas in which families provide services. The first, and most easily calculated in dollars, is material. The family provides basic food, clothing, and shelter to its members. Studies across the board demonstrate the simple fact that if you are married, you are better off financially than if you are single. Not only that, but the responsibilities and tasks of daily life are, at least theoretically, divided by two. In the event of calamity, such as unemployment or illness, there is a human resource to fall back on. Family members will seldom lose their jobs simultaneously; and if you become ill, the chances that you will be able to remain at home increase when you live in a family unit.

The nonmaterial benefits of family are less easily calculated in dollars. Research shows better physical and emotional health among those who are married, compared to those who are not. For example, according to a 1978 study, the death rate due to heart disease was twice as high among divorced men as it was for those who were married. A 1987 study of high blood pressure reported that married people are 20 percent less likely to have high blood pressure than unmarrieds (single, widowed, separated, or divorced). Also, among individuals with high blood pressure, those who were married did better both in seeking treatment and in keeping the condition under control.

The reasons for these differences are less clear than the statistics. Some speculate that better health is due to better nutrition and a healthier life-style among those who are married; perhaps it's easier to grab a snack on the run than cook dinner for only yourself. Others claim it is due primarily to decreased stress among those who are married.

The price tag for the family tasks that could fall to society in cases of divorce involving children is costly. Statistics show that most children live with their mothers after a divorce, and that these women generally suffer a dramatic loss of income, especially in the first year of divorce. The result is that women and children often have need of public monies to take care of themselves. The cost of this support increases annually.

When government-funded studies of love and relationships came under attack by Senator Proxmire in the mid-1970s, James Reston defended them in a *New York Times* article stating, "If the sociologists and psychologists can get even a suggestion of the answer to our pattern of romantic love, marriage, disillusion, divorce...and the children left behind...it would be the best investment of federal money since Jefferson made the Louisiana Purchase."

We hope that the observations and interviews presented in our book will provide part of that answer.